Day After Tomorrow

Day After
TOMORROW

PREPARING
FOR THE
LATER YEARS

By

Roma Rudd Turkel

P. J. KENEDY & SONS
NEW YORK

NIHIL OBSTAT: MARTINUS S. RUSHFORD, PH.D.
                    CENSOR LIBRORUM

IMPRIMATUR: THOMAS EDNUNDUS MOLLOY, S.T.D.
                    ARCHIEPISCOPUS-EPISCOPUS BROOKLYNIENSIS

BROOKLYNII
DIE XX AUGUSTI, 1956

TO MY MOTHER

IT TAKES MANY PEOPLE *to write a book, and I am more grate-ful than I can express to those who shared so intimately the writing of this one: to Father Edward T. Burke for his wise direction and his equally wise deflationary tactics (he taught me a cardinal rule for writers: stop every few pages, and laugh at yourself); to Father Albert A. Murray of the Paulist Fathers for being the most understanding of editors; to Julie Kernan for patiently prodding these chapters out of me; to Alma Savage for backing up good advice with endless cups of good coffee; to my husband for his forbearance; to my boys for putting up with a part-time mother for a while, and espe-cially for the hand-lettered sign which they nailed to my study door while this book was in progress:*

DO NOT DISTRUB FOR ANY
REASON BEFORE 6 PM

Contents

Day After Tomorrow

I

The Bonus Years

THIS IS A BOOK about you and about me and about what is to become of us.

It is a thinking aloud which has resulted from meetings and conversations with many people. Most of them, I think, would be astonished to know that a simple remark, a few words suddenly lighted with joy, or a question carefully skirting an ill-concealed edge of bitterness would help chart a path for the rest of us through those later years from which we seem almost deliberately to turn our minds.

There was the old man I remember who used to spend his days in the park behind New York's public library. He would arrive every morning just before nine, stepping slowly from the swarms of office workers and early shoppers rushing along Forty-second Street. His lunch, later to be shared with the pigeons, was wrapped carefully in a brown paper bag. He would make his way to a sunny bench, and dream the day through. In bad weather he would go into the library and spend the day over a book, though I doubt if he read a word of it. Late in the afternoon he would start watching the big clock opposite the park or the one on the library wall. Promptly at five he would get up, button his worn jacket, and disappear into the homeward-bound crowds.

How many months or years he had lived this routine no one knew until the day some schoolboys started taunting him. A little crowd gathered and a priest who had been taking a short cut through the park walked over to see what was happening. The boys ran away and the crowd melted, but the old man's eyes held the priest.

"Could you spare me a minute, Father?" he asked.

The two sat together on the bench. It took quite a while for the old man to formulate words for what he wanted to say. Apparently it had been a long time since he had talked to anyone.

"Father," he said finally, "it's just that at my age I don't want to be doing anything wrong, and maybe what I'm doing is wrong. I've been spending every day down here, three or four years now. My daughter thinks I have a job. Not a job with pay, because who would pay me? A volunteer job, I told her, so she makes me up a little lunch every morning and gives me carfare, and I spend regular hours here nine to five. She's a good girl and she works hard, and with the children in such a small place, I know it's a relief for her to have me out of the house. And her husband works nights, so he's home days, and he'd just as soon not have me around. Everybody's happier this way, so did I do wrong to tell her I have a job? Besides, as long as they think I have a job, they can't put me in an institution, can they?"

The priest who told me about it didn't tell me the answer he gave. Whatever it was, it was an answer the old man should have had long before he became an old man.

Then there is the wonderful old woman who, if she reads this, will not dream that I am writing about her because she will not recognize herself in the words "old woman." She is old in years and in the infirmities the years bring but younger and more eager in spirit than many young people I know.

All her life has been an outgoing to other people in social service work, in guidance and counseling. She has had no time for problems of her own because she has kept so busy trying to solve those of others.

Now in her eighties, physically unable to continue her active work, she lives alone in a small hall bedroom, just able to meet its modest rent and provide the little food she needs to keep her from day to day. Her room is dark, its one small window into an airshaft providing a kind of twilight at midday. Situated on a noisy street in midtown New York, the place is breathlessly hot all during the city's merciless summer.

She has made countless friends through the years, some of whom have beautiful country places not far from New York, and many of whom have pleasant suburban homes. All of them beg her to spend the summers or a vacation of a few weeks with them. They counter her stubborn refusals with the demand that she at least spend weekends with them to give her a few days' respite from the heat. But she refuses these, too.

To her the reason is simple and makes the best of sense.

"Too many people need me here," she says. "They still come to me with their problems. People can have problems on weekends, too, you know. They know where I am. Wouldn't it be dreadful if they came and didn't find me here?"

Her life is still an outpouring that enriches and strengthens those who come seeking her advice. It is full and satisfying, lighted with the joy that comes from knowing that she is needed.

There are many others: the woman who started happily back to school at seventy-two so she "could help the grandchildren with their home-work," the man whose life was a torment of actual or fancied pains brought about by his forced retirement, the man nearing eighty whose gentle smile could not hide the infinite weariness of his eyes as he said: "We live too long." And there was the unconquerable spirit of the old man who, when asked what an "old person" is, replied: "Anyone who is two years older than I am." Two years later, of course, his reply was the same—and will, I am sure, always be the same.

These and countless others have helped me to write this book. Not the least has been my own family, both its senior and junior members.

My mother does not belong in the "junior" bracket but it is difficult to fit her comfortably into the "senior" bracket, although she is in her seventies. Her interest in everything is both lively and enormous, from household activities to international affairs. She helps my youngest son with his spelling and his piano practice as eagerly as she scans the morning papers for the doings in Washington or watches the progress of the latest French elections.

The world of music in which she has always lived continues to sound around her through recordings and biographies of musicians, composers and conductors she has known. Books are her constant delight, their enjoyment heightened by her rule of rereading a beloved classic between each two new books. She lives alone, yet so full is her home of the musicians and authors, the philosophers and artists of all time that it seems almost an intrusion when we ordinary people visit her, welcome as we know we are.

My mother has her own private joke that furnishes her endless amusement. She is still beautiful, but she laughs whenever she glimpses herself in the mirror.

"It's ridiculous," she declares, "to see that white hair, and those wrinkles. I don't *feel* them. I feel exactly the way I did when I was twenty. I *am* the same person I was then, inside. Why do we have to have mirrors to remind us of the outside changes?"

We ourselves do not see what the mirror sees. To us, she is the same vibrant person she has always been and we need her as much as we ever did.

For a long time I wondered if I would be as interested, and as interesting, at her age. I do not know if I will be, but I am hopeful because I have come to realize that this kind of vital and satisfying old age does not just happen. No kind of old age just happens. It is a normal and natural period of our growth. We grow into it as we grow into adolescence and adulthood and the middle years. We are the same people throughout the whole span, and each period should be the richer for the periods that have gone before.

One of my young sons quite innocently helped me in my thinking. Starting early in October each year, he and his brothers can think, talk, and dream of nothing but Christmas. The excitement mounts feverishly with whispered conferences, hammers banging in the workshop, padlocks on closet doors, and elaborately offhand questions like: "If somebody gave you a tie rack for Christmas, not that anybody would of course because you're a lady, but just say somebody did, could you use it to hang belts and stuff on?"

This year, after the usual three-month whirl of preparations, the day before Christmas came and with it the usual recital of minute-by-minute plans. Spellbound, my youngest listened to plans for Christmas Eve.

"Now tell about tomorrow, Mommy," he said. "Start first thing in the morning and tell everything that will happen all Christmas Day."

When I had done that to the best of my ability, he still was not satisfied.

"Go on, Mommy, go on," he begged. "Now tell about what we're going to do the day *after* tomorrow."

"Why—nothing special," I said. He had taken me by surprise, and I could feel his disappointment at my answer. "Oh," I went on quickly, "you'll play with your toys, and show them to your friends and have a lot of fun."

It was a letdown, I knew. Not that he had expected another Christmas, but he knew that there was another bright new day to come that deserved planning for and that it should not be allowed simply to tag along after the big day.

Isn't that our trouble, I thought—that we spend all our time and energy preparing for the accomplishments of tomorrow's active middle years, and then let the later years tag along after, unplanned and unprepared for. We set our sights too short, and work up feverishly to a letdown.

That is why I hope this thinking aloud will be a thinking together about those later years, which are our common destiny as well as our common blind spot. Because what will become of us tomorrow is not so important as what will become of us the day after tomorrow. Yet tomorrow's prospects are of such absorbing interest to us that all our planning is directed toward them.

Our sense of the future grows as we grow, and should mature as we mature. Infants have no sense of the future. Living entirely in the present, as we shall all live in Heaven, their each experience—a feeding, a cuddling, a warm bath—contains total happiness unmarred by the knowledge that such joys must end. A hunger pang or the sensation of being cold or wet or frightened is total misery, unrelieved by the realization that such conditions will be remedied in time.

As infants grow into young children, their future grows, its bright exploring fingers able to reach at first only as far as the afternoon's walk in the park, or the evening's story-telling. Little by little it can embrace the days ahead—next week's visit to Grandma, next month's birthday. When we are old enough to go to school, our future has grown far enough ahead to savor the delights of next summer's vacation, and perhaps to touch the shining glory of Christmas beyond.

By the time we are in high school we think of college, and begin to plan for the years ahead, blank and beautiful and brimful of exciting promise. Will we be a doctor, a lawyer, an engineer, a teacher? Will we be an actress, a writer, a singer, or perhaps marry a millionaire? Or will we be a priest and have all people as our children to minister to, or a nun wedded to Christ Himself?

God calls these last early, and usually by high school years those He has called have answered. The rest of us keep busy with our dreams into college, and then settle down to intensive preparation for our chosen field. The future stretches ahead of us as far as we can see, but the trouble is that we do not see far enough because we see only tomorrow and not the day after.

We think we see the day after. When we are young, we are willing to admit that we shall one day, God help us, be fifty. We might even be able to look beyond that and grant that we may one day be a senile sixty in a wheel chair. But we do not really believe it. The high excitement and successful accomplishments of the productive middle years blind us to the ones that come after. Time enough, we think, to plan what we'll do when we're approaching retirement age.

What most of us forget is that the later years are not years of doing so much as years of *being*. Being is vastly more important than doing. It is the kind of person we are, the kind of person we grow to be through all our busy years, that makes the later years rich and rewarding, or lonely and bitter.

Where and on what scale we shall live when our active years are over, what income we shall have, how we shall occupy our time, are specifics which should be planned during our middle years. But the kind of person we shall be then is the kind we must start cultivating purposefully during our twenties and thirties.

I have often wondered why it is that none of us likes to look beyond tomorrow. Why do most of us close our eyes and our minds to the days when we shall no longer be young and vigorous and physically attractive? If we think those years may be unpleasant, and it is a human failing to shy away from unpleasant things, we are not using the common sense the good Lord gave us and realizing that just as we can make ourselves into successful doctors or merchants or housewives, we can make ourselves into successful old people.

I think we may be confused by much that has been said, particularly during recent years when our increasing life span has brought the problem of the aged into sharp perspective. Our later years, which should be our crowning years, have been described in oddly conflicting ways. They are called "the lonely years," and they are called "the golden years." They are neither. They need not be lonely, unless we deliberately make them so. And they will be no more (and no less) golden than our earlier years, because they are part of life. And though life has its golden moments, which sometimes stretch into hours and days, all of life is not unalloyed gold. Each age has problems of its own. The problems of old age are no more severe than those of adolescence or the middle years. They simply are different.

I like to think of them as the quiet years, all the quiet minutes and hours I promise myself but never manage to get in the rush of a busy office and a busier household, saved for me—with interest added—to savor and enjoy when the rush is over. Time to think and time to pray. Time to love and be loved.

But of course we shall have to start filling the bank of our later years now or we shall find it empty then. It will not be the quiet time I have longed for if I am beset by fears and plagued by bitterness, if I have become narrowed and alone, turned in upon myself to taste the final loneliness.

There will be no point in having time to think if I have nothing to think about. Time to pray will be despair if I have not spent my growing years learning to know and love and serve God, so that I can talk to Him easily and gratefully in those later years when I am in His anteroom and, more importantly, listen to Him and learn those things I still must learn if I am to open the right door. Time to love will be empty unless I have spent a lifetime loving. And only if I have done that will I be loved.

I remember a priest telling me of the time when, as a young man only two or three years out of the seminary, he was called to the bedside of an old man who was dying. The old man knew he had but a few minutes more, and as he grasped the priest's hand his sunken eyes shone.

"Father," he said, in a simple and joyous summing-up of his life, "I have been faithful to my marriage."

The young priest was not particularly impressed by what the old man said. It was commendable, he thought, a fine thing, and something which apparently made the old man happy at the last. But through the years, what he had heard penetrated ever deeper into the priest's heart, until he came to recognize it as the finest accounting that can be given of a married person's life, and the only accounting important in Heaven. Instinctively, as life loosened its hold, the old man had been able to put first things first. In those moments, none of the other successes of his long life mattered; important as they were to him at the time, they had faded into forgetfulness. Only his vocation, his marriage, the road God had set him upon to reach Heaven, stood out clear and shining in his mind. He had been faithful to it. It was enough. He was ready to meet God Who had asked it of him.

Getting to Heaven is neither confusing nor complicated. There are three roads, and only three, that lead there: the single life in religion, the single life in the world and the married life. God has set each of us on one of the three and His directions are crystal-clear: "Follow this road to eternal happiness with Me in Heaven." It does not matter how popular or respected we are among our companions along the road, or how unknown or even despised we find ourselves. All that matters is that we follow the road, shunning detours and tempting bypaths. It is enough, when we reach the end, that we are able to say: "I have been faithful to my priesthood," "I have been faithful to my vows," "I have been faithful, Lord, to the single life in the world for which You set me the example," or, as the old man said so joyously, "I have been faithful to my marriage."

I am often tempted to think of myself as many things besides a wife and mother. It is not because people toss bones to us wives and mothers and try to keep us content with a "your work is important *too*, dear," that I have sought and met so many challenges outside my home. I have found the advertising business exciting and exhilarating through the years. I find creative joy and deep satisfaction in writing. I find lecturing a stimulating and happy experience. I love working with teen agers, especially problem ones. Every day is packed to overflowing with things to be done, and my many failures are quickly forgotten in the radiance of my few successes.

I have to keep reminding myself that none of these things is of the least importance when the chips are down. When I am called upon to give an accounting, there will be no carbon copies of what I have written, no photostats of my advertising campaigns, no tape recordings of my lectures. I can take with me only what I am, not what I have or have done. I will be asked: "What kind of wife and mother have you been?" It bears much thinking about, and I am grateful for the prospect of quiet years ahead when I can think about it.

We have so many more years to look forward to than did our parents. People are living longer today, and will live even longer tomorrow, thanks to the comparatively new science of geriatrics, increased medical knowledge and the "wonder" drugs. Our life span has increased more than twenty years in the last half century alone.

What shall we do with these bonus years? Where shall we put them? Shall we use them to multiply our active, productive middle years? Or will they be added on to our later years when the pace slows down and self-support largely ceases? The answer depends upon individual circumstances. If the work we do calls for retirement at a fixed age regardless of our ability, if we have not trained ourselves to do some sort of work which interests us and which we can do after such forced retirement, or if our health curtails our active years, the bonus years still stretch ahead. If our work is the kind that can be continued as long as we are able to do it and find enjoyment in it, and if we have taken good care of our health, the bonus years can be productive years.

Whatever we do with them, the bonus years have been given us. The tragedy of the old man who said, "We live too long," is a self-imposed one, the tragedy of finding the bonus years empty because they were not prepared for.

We see evidence of the bonus years on every hand, splitting the seams of our hospitals and homes for the aged, crowding our houses and apartments, alerting doctors, social workers, welfare groups, insurance companies, municipal and federal agencies.

During the last fifty years the population in this country has doubled, but the number of people over sixty-five has increased almost four times. By 1975, it is predicted, about twenty million Americans will be over sixty-five.

I shall be over sixty-five then, and perhaps you will be too.

Sixty-five, of course, is an arbitrary figure. It has been generally accepted as the "start of old age" because it is the age at which compulsory retirement is most often set in business and industry. There is no reason why the start of old age shouldn't be set at seventy, eighty or ninety. On the other hand, it could quite legitimately be set at forty, when our physical powers begin to decline, or even on the morning of our twenty-sixth birthday when, according to many people, we have taken the first step past our prime.

Actually, we are born with the capabilities and potentials, in seed form, that will grow into the kind of people we will become. Today, whatever our age, we are unfinished. Tomorrow we shall still be unfinished. But the day after we shall see the results of our strivings. What is more, we shall live the results, joyously or bitterly, according to how we have wrought them. We shall be what we are now becoming.

It is not too soon to begin planning because, like all the days of our life, the day after tomorrow is only a preparation for the day after *that*. That is the big day that cannot be planned, the day that will be the happiest or the bitterest of all, depending entirely upon the kind of people we have made of ourselves.

II

The Unmarked Roads

I HAVE ALWAYS been fascinated by travelers' tales of certain natives in India who can die at will. When they have no longer any desire to live, the story goes, they lie down and turn their faces to the wall and die.

They are supposed to be able to do this, regardless of their age or the state of their health, simply by willing to die. Like the famous Indian rope trick, it is impossible to find anyone who has actually seen it done, so we are entitled to any skepticism we may have. But the stories persist, and although we cannot prove them true, neither can we prove them untrue. With all our research, we have barely been able to pry beneath the surface of our physical and spiritual powers, and the few facts of which we have experimental knowledge are as nothing to the vast body of facts of which we have no knowledge at all.

Perhaps these natives have trained their will power to the point where they are able to command what are normally instinctive actions, and thus are able to stop breathing when they wish. Or perhaps they are able to put themselves into an apparently lifeless trance until the gullible traveler has rushed out to spread his remarkable tale.

There is, however, a nugget of truth hidden in their action if not in its result. In order to "die," they turn their faces to the wall, turning from family and friends in a final deliberate choice of loneliness.

It is significant that loneliness is the greatest single problem of those of us who reach the later years. As scientific studies dig ever more deeply into the problems of those years, it is emerging as a greater threat than we dreamed. Loneliness may someday be proved to be the number-one killer of the aged because it shrivels their spirit and kills their will to live. It destroys their defenses, and leaves them helpless against the onset and ravages of disease. Without the will to live, even the "wonder" drugs are virtually powerless. Doctors are first to tell us that the mental attitudes of old people have much to do with their physical ills and with the results of physical treatment.

But loneliness, although it is the thing we have to fear most about the day after tomorrow, is happily the easiest to prevent. It need not happen. Only the old who have let it happen know what loneliness is.

We think we know. We may feel lonely now, or remember times when we have felt lonely, but the all-alone feelings we sometimes experience are as different from true loneliness as a cinder in the eye is from blindness.

I can remember many times when I have felt miserably lonely. Most recent was a rainy night in a hotel, midway on a lecture tour and a thousand miles from home. I knew no one in the city, I missed my family, I had a cold coming on and no one to be concerned about it. My next day's audience would have been astounded if they had seen their lecturer bawling like a baby just because she felt lonely and sorry for herself. I finally decided to make a shambles of the expense account and telephone home, to hear a few friendly words. I did phone, and the words were friendly enough, but they were not quite so enthusiastic as I had hoped, because

I had forgotten the difference in time and had pulled my hard-working husband out of bed and downstairs at three in the morning.

Even children know these all-alone feelings. There was the little boy who wrote a pitiful letter home from summer camp, saying how lonely he was. His distressed parents phoned him immediately.

"How can you be lonely, Jimmy," they asked, "with all those other boys in your cabin?"

"Oh," said Jimmy, "they're all lonely too."

Like Jimmy, we know what the word is supposed to mean, but we have not experienced its meaning.

Our feelings of loneliness, however miserable, are bearable because we know they are temporary. We know there are people who love us and who need us, people for whom we care and in whom we are interested, people to whom we are important and who would miss us if we were no longer here. We may be separated from them by distance or by misunderstanding, but both distance and misunderstanding can be bridged. Each man may be an island, but if he has many bridges leading to and from his island, and if he keeps his bridges open and in good repair, he can never be lonely.

True loneliness is a fearsome thing. Only those who experience it can know its total despair. But it is important for us who do not yet know it to try to peer into its depths now, because the roads that lead to loneliness have their beginnings in our active years, and they are not marked.

We must first distinguish between aloneness and loneliness. They are not the same. Aloneness is a physical experience, that of being by oneself. Loneliness is a spiritual experience, that of being abandoned. A person who is alone need never be lonely. To be physically alone because of circumstances does not limit the spirit, but can instead send it on even more eager missions of love and understanding and helpfulness to others whether they live around the block or around the world.

To be physically alone can be a hardship, but it can also be an opportunity if we have built up resources within us. Solitude can make saints of us if we use it as we should. Its danger is that we may concentrate our attention upon ourselves and so go down the road to loneliness. Its opportunity lies in the quiet uninterrupted time it gives us to know God better and to feel His love filling us so full that we can no longer contain it but must lavish it upon others by whatever means we have.

Perhaps that is why the opportunity of solitude may some day be given to those of us who have been too busy during our active years to give a thought to God, or to set aside quiet times to find Him.

All our lives we have had His clear direction before us: *Be still and know that I am God*. How dense can we be, not to understand a simple eight-word command, phrased in one-syllable words? How obstinate can we be in refusing to take Him literally? He means just what He says: first we have to *be still;* then and only then shall we *know*. We come to a certain knowledge of God only in silence and solitude. That may be why so many of us run from both, and fill our ears and our hours with chatter and clutter. And perhaps that is why some of us may have to be taken by the figurative scruff of our necks and deposited in silence and solitude so that we may learn what we must learn before it is too late.

Just as a person who is alone need not be lonely, so a person can be lonely with many people around him. The old man who once told me, "We live too long," knew loneliness in the midst of a busy household. He felt that he was in the way and unwanted, and spent his days talking to himself because there was no one who took the trouble to talk to him.

One of the loneliest old women I ever knew lived amid the bustle of a busy modern hospital and home for the aged. Every type of activity and therapy suited to her needs was available, and she was constantly encouraged to participate. Entertainment and companionship flowed around her, but she made no response. For a long time, possibly for years, she watched the others, her great dark eyes remote and without luster, seeming to stare out of the abyss of loneliness into which she was sinking. Then she took to keeping her eyes closed for long periods, with an occasional tear coursing down the furrows of her cheeks. One day her eyes closed for the last time, and it was not until two hours later that they discovered she was dead. There did not seem to be a great deal of difference, because loneliness itself is a living death.

Loneliness is the inner conviction that we are no longer needed, no longer wanted, no longer loved. Imagine, if you can, the crushing despair of knowing that there is no one, anywhere, who has the slightest interest in whether you live or die. Imagine the hopelessness of feeling without value to anyone, and therefore without value to yourself.

You sit alone, unwanted, useless. No one comes seeking your help, your advice, your opinions, or even your conversation. No one comes seeking *you*, because you no longer exist for others or, if you do, it is only as a burden. You have nothing to look forward to, no prospect but waiting out the lonely days, no hope that conditions will ever change, no reason you can see for being alive. You begin to feel that you are in the way and that others resent the little care that you require, the little food you eat and the little space you occupy, even your very presence. Your mind begins to run down dark and twisted channels, wondering if and when their resentment will impel them to rid themselves of such a burden—whether by positive means or by sheer neglect.

You begin to wonder if you should not save them the trouble. You become secretive and suspicious, and turn in upon yourself to find the final loneliness.

Old people, when they have closed off outside interests and outgoing contacts, focus their attention inward. They watch their bodies slowing down and become sorry for themselves. They magnify the natural infirmities of old age. Fancied slights grow enormous and demands for attention inordinate. As self-pity grows, so do complaints and the actual aggravation of physical ills—for they cling subconsciously to these physical ills as their only means of getting the attention they crave. Thus they become more difficult, more demanding, more of a care. And so the problem grows.

Loneliness, in a very real sense, is hell. A spirit can live and grow only when it is turned upward and outward, loving God and living that love in selfless service to others. When it turns in upon itself it finds nothingness, and must shrivel and die. Hell must be very much like that—a place of utter, despairing loneliness where the knowledge that we are abandoned by God is infinitely bitter because we know that we are the ones who did the abandoning.

C. S. Lewis in his book *The Great Divorce*, which tells the story of an imaginary bus trip from hell to Heaven, describes hell in a way that gives a vivid picture of its loneliness. Hell, as he pictures it in his fantasy, is an endless and dismal town where it is always raining and always gloomy with a twilight that never deepens into night. Night would cover its misery, and night would give way to morning, but misery is forever there and morning never breaks in hell. The gray houses stretch out, street by lonely street, to infinity. The inhabitants are so quarrelsome, a resident explains, that when a newcomer arrives from earth and settles down, he quarrels so badly with his neighbors that he keeps moving from street to street until he builds a house on the edge of town. From there he keeps moving farther and farther away, and thus the town keeps growing.

Lewis asks about people who arrived in hell long ago, and the resident tells him that they are still moving and getting astronomical distances apart. If he uses a powerful telescope he is just able to see the lights of some of the inhabited houses, millions of miles away and millions of miles from each other, where the old ones live in such loneliness and bitterness that they still keep moving.

Loneliness is hell, but it is a hell of our own making. We cannot experience it accidentally, but only deliberately—just as no one finds himself in hell except by his own deliberate choice. He might not choose hell if given his choice at the end, but he will not be given that choice because he has already chosen his destination in countless decisions during his lifetime. Nor would we choose loneliness during our later years. If it should be our lot, it will be a self-imposed one, the sum of a hundred choices we have made during our active years and the end of a hundred unmarked roads into which we have turned because of what seemed, at the time, sufficient reason.

As the years multiply, they keep emptying themselves of friends and of interests. Unless we keep refilling them with new friends and new interests, there will be a narrowing of life about us until we find ourselves, one day, alone within the shell of our years.

Our friends die one by one or they move away, and whether they move across the city or across the world makes little difference to an old person whose physical activity is limited. Business and social acquaintances drop off as our active years slow down and we find ourselves not only without the activities which kept those years busy but without the people who helped keep them bright.

Have you noticed how people, sometimes during their

forties, start reading the obituary columns in the newspapers? It is not, as someone once suggested, for the happy surprise of not finding themselves listed. It is because they know they are at an age when the ranks of their contemporaries start thinning out and, consciously or not, they seek the daily reassurance of finding no familiar names on the list. They themselves may have good reason to feel that another forty years or more stretch before them, and they may not yet be conscious of a decline in their physical faculties. But the decline has commenced, the cutting-down to size has begun; in a dozen hidden ways it stabs at their sense of security which they seek to bolster even with such straws as obituary lists made up of strangers.

The roads which lead off from our active years to loneliness in the later ones are not marked, or of course we should never take them. They seem to run quietly alongside our busy highway, and in the same direction so that we assume their destination to be the same. Their beginnings are pleasant, and tempt us to step out of the rush. If they are less populated, and taking them means leaving some of our friends, we feel that they will at least be restful and therefore good for us. What we do not realize is that nothing is better for us than our friends, and that our day after tomorrow will be bleak indeed if we have not held firmly to every friend we have, and made new ones to take the places of those who must slip from our grasp.

Each Christmas for several years I was tempted into one of those side roads until I realized what was happening. Each year, faced with my staggering and ever-growing Christmas card list, I'd vow to cut it down. I had never been one to trade card for card, to keep a record of who failed to send me a card and cross him off the list the following year. No one was ever crossed off, and everyone I met during the year was added to the list the following Christmas. It has always been a joy to me to spread the Good Tidings, and to greet everyone I know on the birthday of Him Who first greeted us.

But as the list grew longer it became more and more expensive and took up more and more time and energy that I thought I could not afford. I was busy in so many ways, many of them ways to add to the joy of Christmas at home, that seemed of more immediate importance.

So each year I'd sharpen a pencil and sit down with a firm: "I'm going to cut this list down to fifty—or seventy-five at the most." But I never knew where to start. Should I cut out all those I did not remember having heard from for a few years? Or should I cut out all business acquaintances and leave in only people I knew socially? Or should I cut from the social list all except close friends so that I could squeeze in a few business acquaintances who seemed important to me?

It was the third or fourth Christmas, I think, that I had tried without success to cut the list down, when I realized what I was doing. As I sat chewing my pencil and weighing each name, something made me think of the sheep and the goats, the wheat and the chaff. There I was like the Avenging Angel (my husband said I had just as black a scowl) trying to decide who was and who was not worthy of being on my list. I was trying to cut off the lifelines of communication I would one day need so much, trying to burn all but a few bridges to my little island. Some day I would wonder why my island was so lonely, and remember bitterly the bridges I had destroyed because their upkeep took a little effort. It was the first tempting step down one of the roads to loneliness, and I am thankful I stepped back in time.

There are many of these roads to tempt us as the years

pile up to tire us. Some of them beckon even earlier, before enough years have accumulated to slow us down, and it is selfishness that urges us to take them.

Very early comes the road that suggests we drop certain friends in order to adopt others who may be more advantageous to us. During college years we are tempted to drop those of our friends who were forced to end their formal education with high school. We have progressed to a different "class," we think, and college contacts are much more valuable.

During early business years, as we rise through the ranks, we feel that we should drop those we left behind. The girl who steps out of the stenographic pool to become a private secretary fancies that there are disadvantages in her continued association with those left paddling in the pool. The young man promoted from stock boy to clerk looks down upon his former friends. Given a few years and a promotion to office manager, he will set his sights on a district managership, and prefer scotch with the "brass" to beer with the crowd he used to enjoy.

These early roads to loneliness have exciting beginnings. They seem to be expressways to speed us to our goal by by-passing ordinary slow-moving traffic. Later roads have different beginnings to appeal to our changing pace. They become more leisurely and restful in appearance, beckoning us out of the rush "for our own good."

Like the one that urged me to cut down my Christmas card list, there are others that suggest we stop visiting friends who have moved from the neighborhood. "It's an hour's drive out to Suburbia," we reason, "and that means a two-hour round trip. Maybe three, with the traffic. It will take too much out of us. Besides, it will put them under obligation to come in and see us, so we're really being considerate of them by not going." We begin refusing invitations because we'd rather relax at home by ourselves, and because of the effort involved in returning the hospitality of the friends whose invitations we accept.

A man becomes loath to budge from armchair and television after a busy day, forgetting that when his busy days are over the business acquaintances who filled them will be gone too, and there will be no others to replace them. A woman begins to cut down or cut out her service activities—bowing out as entertainment chairman of her parish organization, secretary of the woman's club, girl scout leader or cub scout den mother, collector for the Red Cross or the mothers' drive against polio. Her "I'm getting on, you know, and must conserve my energy," is an excellent excuse. But, unless her health really makes it necessary, she may find that what she cuts out is of far greater value to her than what she conserves.

There is a private road that branches off during our middle years, and it is especially tempting because it is limited to ourselves and our long-time friends. We find the companionship of those we have known over the years to be easy and comfortable, and begin to resist the idea of meeting new people. The effort it takes to get to know them, to search for a common ground of interest, to put our best foot forward so that they will appreciate us as much as do our old friends—it tires us to think of the whole process, and we doubt that it would be worth-while.

We become particularly reluctant to meet younger people and to set about cultivating their friendship. It may be that during these years when our eyesight starts becoming fuzzy, our insight does the same. Many of our oldest friends will not continue to be with us for a long time. We shall need replacements, particularly among younger people who at least stand a better chance of being around as long as we are. And we shall very much need, all our lives, the challenge of fresh ideas and opinions and personalities with which new friendships stimulate and enlarge our own spirit.

These and the hundred other roads to loneliness are not marked, but they are easy to recognize because they have one thing in common: they lead us away from people. We may some day find it necessary or wise to cut down on our activities, but it is never necessary, and can be dangerously unwise, to cut down on people.

People are a living insurance for the quiet years ahead. I like to think of my friends as a fund that I am building now for those years, and check every little while to make sure that the fund is growing steadily, and that the deposits far exceed the withdrawals.

Friends, in themselves, cannot prevent loneliness in the later years, because loneliness is an inner experience which can be prevented only by turning and growing upward and outward. The old woman I met in the hospital and home for the aged was surrounded by friends eager to help her—yet she died of loneliness. We must remember that we shall need friends in the years ahead, not because of what they can do for us, but because of what we can do for them.

We shall need to be needed in those years, to make them full and joyous. We shall be needed if we avoid the unmarked roads, and make today and tomorrow a purposeful expanding of our friendships and a selfless giving of ourselves to our friends so that, on the day after tomorrow, our friends will know they need us and come flocking.

III

Questions Ahead

When I was sixteen, I read a story called "Letter to Alicia," though who wrote it and where I read it I have long forgotten. It was the story of a woman on her fortieth birthday reading a letter that she had written to herself when she was sixteen. The idea intrigued me because I was the same age, so I promptly sat down and wrote a letter to "Dear Roma-at-forty," sealed it carefully and tucked it away where I hoped it would be safe through the years.

I thought of it when I turned forty. The letter itself had disappeared amid the mayhem of a busy household and the weeding-out of many movings, but I remembered it, particularly the opening sentence: "Now that the romance and excitement are over, and you can look back at it all, what has your life been like?"

The whoop of laughter I gave, as I remembered, brought my boys running. I'm sure they were convinced, as I had been at sixteen, that when people reach forty senility sets in and all sorts of silly things are to be expected.

Romance? Excitement? Poor little sixteen-year-old, pitying me from the depths of her own fears and uncertainties and confusion. She felt reasonably sure that I would be alive at forty, but scarcely more than alive—certainly not a type of aliveness that she would call living. But though I can laugh at her, and feel sorry for her too, she could not possibly have understood, just as I cannot hope to make a present-day youngster understand, that romance and excitement heighten and deepen with maturity beyond her wildest dreams, and that the full rushing river of life is something that cannot be imagined by one who is enchanted by the trickling stream of its beginning.

I remember that the rest of the letter was filled with eager curiosity. Was I happy, and what had made me happiest? Was I married, and was my husband handsome? How many children did I have? Where did I live, in what kind of house? Was I rich? What did I find to do with myself in the sunset of life? I remember that "sunset of life" expression vividly, as well as another question that had been underlined: *Does it feel awful to be forty?*

No, dear, it feels fine to be forty, I thought, and if this is the sunset of life it's the brightest sunset I ever saw. More like high noon, with all the whistles blowing. There's a busy afternoon ahead, and an exciting evening beyond. You, back there in the morning, with your scrubbed face and your school books, the best and most wonderful thing I can wish you is to be forty and find out for yourself!

Now, remembering that letter, I am intrigued all over again by the idea of writing another one to "Dear Roma-at-seventy." And I suspect when I am seventy and think of the letter I wrote during these middle years, I will laugh just as heartily—and feel a little sorry, too, for myself in my forties. For though seventy seems to me now to be deep in the quiet twilight years, I may well feel then that it is only a little past noon, with the whistles still sounding in my ears.

I may think now that there is nothing more full and more satisfying than the rushing river I am trying to navigate, but that is because the river is all I know. I have had no experience of the wide calm sea toward which the river is rushing.

Because I have never known the sea, the expression "when the rush is over" must mean to me only that the river itself stops rushing, slows down and becomes stagnant and finally dries up. Those who know the delights and the depths of the sea, bright and broad as the sky it reflects, abounding with life and pushing its ripples to the farthest shores, must pity us who ask: "But what is left when the river stops rushing?"

If I were to write that letter to myself-at-seventy, I'm sure I'd be just as curious as a sixteen-year-old. The questions would not be too different.

I know I would start with the same: "Are you happy, and what has made you happiest?" I would not have to ask if my husband is handsome, because he was handsome when I married him and has been getting handsomer through the years; white hair should be his crowning glory. And I wouldn't have to ask how many children I have, though I should most certainly be eager to know about my grandchildren and great-grandchildren.

I think I'd be a little more practical about the other questions. Where do you live, I'd ask—independently, in a place of your own? Or do you live with one of the children? Have you perhaps decided on group living in some community planned and geared for old people? Or do you live in a home for the aged? Wherever you live, how and why did you come to the decision to live there?

I'm sure I would not ask if I were rich—that is, rich in money. Even now I have neither the expectation nor the desire for wealth. Money is a lovely commodity, and it is mighty handy to have as much of it as you need for what you need, with a few comforts now and then, but having a great surplus imposes an even greater responsibility. I should, however, ask some questions about money. What sort of income do you have, I would want to know. How did you arrange to have such an income? Is it enough for your needs? Or are you partially or totally dependent upon others? Must you still earn money in order to live?

The prospect of still having to earn an income in those days would stir up another batch of questions: How are you earning a living? Are you able to continue your present work, though perhaps in modified form? Or were you able to transpose the skills and experience of your present work into another field where no arbitrary age limit makes them unacceptable? Did a present hobby grow into an unexpected income-producer? Or did you develop new skills to support you?

What do you *do* with yourself, I would want to know, and even now I can hear a whoop of laughter down the years, not gentle as you'd expect seventy-year-old laughter to be, but a riotous burst of it. I can almost hear the reply: "Enough questions—I've promised the publishers three chapters by Friday, there's a magazine deadline on the fifteenth, Christopher and his wife are bringing the great-grandchildren over for dinner, and if I don't get the pot roast on now they'll be gnawing on raw meat. Even these new-fangled solar ranges need a full ten minutes if you like your meat well done."

I would wonder about health, too. How have you been cut down to size, I would want to know, and how much? Are you still physically active, or are you confined to your room or perhaps to your bed? Did any of the little ills and ailments that I too often neglect now, in the rush, grow into big ones? Did the mounting tensions of these busy years explode into incapacitating physical ills? And my curiosity would push my impertinence to the point of asking: Did you ever manage to get your weight down or are you now overflowing two rocking chairs?

I think I would be most curious of all about God's

nearness. It will not be too long before you meet Him, I would write. How do you feel about that meeting? Are you eager for it, or a little frightened? I think I would hear a laugh again, but a more gentle one this time. I think I would hear the answer: "You can't be frightened of a Friend." At least I hope I would, because then I would know that my life, busy or not, had become a conversation with Him. And when one is enjoying such a conversation, one notices neither how time passes nor when it has passed forever, because the conversation keeps on going.

It is more than a fanciful idea; it is immensely practical for each of us to write such a letter to ourselves in our later years—provided we don't save it to open then. The time to answer its questions is now. Of course some of them cannot be answered fully because of factors we cannot foresee, but most of them must be answered during our active years if the answers are to be the ones we choose, rather than be left to chance and circumstance.

We'll want to do some thinking together about how to make the day after tomorrow a happy one, about where we will live and how we will feel, and about how we will manage to support ourselves if necessary. We will want to think about what we will do, but most of all we will want to think about what we will be. If we are the right kind of people, it won't matter much what we do because what we do will flow from what we are. All of it will be happy and satisfying to us and to those around us, because we shall have discovered how wonderfully true it is that "to those who love God, all things work together unto good."

The first question in your letter will most probably be, as mine was, "Are you happy, and what has made you happiest?"

If we could hear the answer it might surprise us, because our ideas of happiness change and grow as we do. If I had told my sixteen-year-old self why I am happy today, she would not have understood, and now I find myself amazed at the things that made her happy. How could the sum of happiness in those days have consisted of an embarrassed "hello" from the blond boy in the next block, or being chosen for the knobby-kneed lead in the school play, or being invited to a football game by a *college man* and being able to look down my nose at friends who had had to be satisfied with high school boys as escorts?

I think I know the things that make me happy today, but I think too that I may be wrong. It takes a lot of living to sift out the values, and some day I'll no doubt wonder at the unimportance of the things that make me happy now, and at the even greater unimportance of the things that distress me. I'll know then that real, rock-solid happiness consists not in living and doing, but in living and doing for others—and that problems should not distress me because they have a purpose, and all God's purposes are good.

But if I am to be happy in those years, I must do more now than merely avoid the roads that lead to loneliness. I must do something more positive than simply taking care not to limit my friends or turn my life away from people—I must be alert for opportunities to keep them, and to keep them increasing.

All through life these opportunities keep nudging us. Being the busy preoccupied people we are, perhaps they should shout, or beat us about the head to attract our attention. But they don't, they just nudge, and we usually shrug them off.

"I wonder what ever happened to Betty Smith, that nice receptionist who left the office a couple of years ago to get married?" we ask.

But it is only a nudge. We are too busy to bother about Betty, much as we liked her, so we shrug off the opportunity.

Perhaps Betty is tied down with a baby and a home to care for, and would welcome a visitor and a "coffee break" to talk over old times. Perhaps we could baby sit for her occasionally, and give her a chance to do some needed shopping or enjoy an evening out with her husband. Perhaps she is ill, or looking for a job, or in need of our help in any one of a dozen ways. But it is too late; we have dismissed Betty as an idle thought, and the opportunity will not come again.

"Well, look at this—Joe Smith has his name in the paper. Seems he's working for a company out in Denver now, and one of his suggestions saved the plant a lot of money. He was always smart, Joe was. Must be ten years since he left town—I often wondered what became of him."

We get a little nudge to write to Joe and congratulate him on his award. No hurry about it, of course; the fights are on television tonight, and then we will have to turn in because tomorrow is going to be a rough day. So, sometime during the evening's fights or the rough next day, we lose Joe and the opportunity of helping him. Perhaps we don't see how we could help him, but with Joe as with the rest of us one of the biggest helps is just knowing that we are remembered.

We get these nudges every day. If we acted only upon those we felt during the course of a single week, we should be different and better people and find the results out of all proportion to the small effort they cost: the telephone call, the friendly note. If we made a habit of acting upon our nudges, of seizing all the little opportunities for growth that bombard us, we would be lighting our later years with the warmth of friendship and the joy of being needed.

Some years ago I read a magazine article which moved me greatly.

"I'd like to write to the man who wrote this," I said, "and tell him how much I think of it."

"Why don't you?" asked my husband.

"Ridiculous," I said. "I've never written to a stranger in all my life."

But I wrote, and because I knew something about the subject of the article, I was able to add some of my own experiences and opinions. My answer was a three-page, single-spaced letter which grew into a stimulating correspondence over the years, and finally to a meeting and a friendship which my husband and I have cherished ever since.

Actually, that chance letter has widened our circle by more than one, because several of the author's friends are now our friends too. And that chance letter did more. The author persuaded me to rewrite my original letter to him into an article, and suggested a magazine that might be interested. It was my first published piece, and started me on the writing that has been one of my greatest joys ever since.

That first experience encouraged me to write another letter of appreciation to a nun who teaches at a school in the midwest. I had enjoyed an article of hers, and wanted to tell her so. I was surprised and delighted when her reply told me how much she had enjoyed an article of *mine*. We have never met but I feel that we are close friends, and her lively letters help light the day for me when they arrive.

A woman I know walked into a strange house one day to make a friend. She had often passed the house on her way to church, and had noticed an old woman who seemed to be always looking out one of the front windows. On an impulse she stopped in one morning. The old woman's welcome was shy but warm.

"I keep seeing you going over to church," she said in broken English. "It would be so nice to go again, for me. The church was near once, but now it is very far away since my leg got so stiff and slow and all the way feels uphill."

"Suppose I come for you in the car," my friend said. "Would you come with me? I'd love to have someone to go with."

The old woman was delighted, not only with the opportunity of getting to church once more, but with my friend's implied need of her companionship.

Over the months more elderly people along the way have become regular and happy passengers, but I think my friend is the happiest of the car load. She has made good friends of their families, too. Now that she is planning a trip to Italy in the spring, the old woman whose solitary figure in the window started it all is enthusiastically teaching her Italian. The lessons, punctuated by giggles and livened by stories of the old woman's girlhood near Milan, are highlights of the week for both of them.

A child acts impulsively, and we should think it quite natural of him, once he is out of range of our inhibiting presence, to walk into a strange house and say "hello" to a strange old woman, as my friend did. We have seen children walk up to people they have never seen before, and win them with a trusting, "I like you," which was what I said, in effect, to make new friends of those to whom I wrote: "I like what you write." It took a little effort for me to write those letters, during busy days when there were so many more pressing things to be done, but my reward was great and will keep growing greater. During the quiet years ahead, I see no limit to the friendships I can make. I feel them ahead of me, beckoning and eager, awaiting only the days when I have more time to send my spirit adventuring.

A child doesn't stop to question the source of his impulses, or weigh their probable worth. He accepts them, acts upon them and so his world expands because they are impulses to growth. As his spirit grows it keeps nudging him on, urging him to ask questions the livelong day, to explore new places and learn new things, to welcome everyone as a friend and to let them know in simple honesty that he is their friend.

We never outgrow these spiritual nudges, these impulses to growth, we only ignore them. They usually come when we are busy or tired, and we have a hundred excuses for not acting upon them. But if we are to become as little children, our spirit growing and expanding like theirs as our physical world is made small again, we must respond to good impulses as they do.

I have a theory that is far from scientific, and may be equally far from being good theology. It may, too, be unjust to many old people, so that I should feel more comfortable in speaking of it if it went in one ear and out the other and did not linger in the process. But since it is mine, and since I believe in it and so far have found no reason to discard it, perhaps I will be forgiven any injustice that may be done in mentioning it.

I have often been struck, and forcefully, by the sharp difference in attitude there is among old people with respect to children. There seem to be no halfway attitudes, no take-it-or-leave-it kind of tolerance. All the old people I have met, and I have met many, seem to fall into just two classes: those who delight in young children, and those who can't stand them.

We have all seen old people who delight in youngsters. The two seem to have a natural affinity, speak the same language but need no words for perfect understanding, enjoy the same things and find their greatest pleasure in enjoying them together. The old person may not be able to explain why, after an adult lifetime, he feels so at home with the little ones. A child doesn't seek an explanation, but knows with the certainty of the truth by which he lives that

Grandpa is "his kind" and not a grownup like Mommy and Daddy and their friends.

I believe that old people like these are ready, or almost ready, for Heaven. They have become children again in spirit. They have cleared away the encrustations of the years, and truth has taken possession of them and filled them with simplicity and innocence and love. Children cannot be deceived. A child recognizes a kindred spirit, and thinks no more of white hair and glasses and grown-up clothes than he would of a Halloween costume.

We have also seen people who do not like having children around. They shoo them off. They become irritated at their questions, enraged at the noise they make, furious at a clutter of toys underfoot. When the occasion demands conversation with a child, as when friends come calling with their offspring, what these old people have to say is both brief and awkward. They have, in fact, nothing to say to a child, because they have nothing in common with him. The child knows, and is silent and embarrassed. Sometimes he is frightened and tries to escape because he knows that he is confronted by a stranger who is really strange. This strange person is not a child, and he is not even a grownup like Mommy and Daddy. He is a grownup who has grown far away in another direction, and he is dark inside. He is bad.

"He is bad" is a child's conclusion, not mine. My possible injustice to old people who do not like children is believing that, though they may have been cut to child size by physical infirmities, their spirits are still too overgrown and bulky with encrustations to fit the Children's Entrance, that little door that is the only entrance to Heaven.

I can guess as I look at them that they have not much time left, and I am torn with pity at the picture of their struggles when they try to squeeze through so small a door and find they cannot. One of the most important things about that door is that it is always open. The sight beyond will be a joy to those who can walk through. To those who cannot, it will be a sight to torture them forever, remembering where they might be if they had only known.

The little nudges that urge us to the kindnesses that keep our friends needing us and bring others to us in ever-increasing numbers keep enlarging our spirit to child size because they are practices in selfless love. We may be impatient with them at first, as we were with scales on the piano or the first declension in our Latin grammar, but if we persist in our response they will become a habit that will transform our later years.

Lighted and warmed with that kind of love, it will not very much matter where or how we live the day after tomorrow. If circumstances give us no choice as to where we shall live, what we shall do, how dependent upon others we shall be, we shall at least know that we can never be a burden, nor unwanted, nor lonely.

But most of us are given choices, back in our active years, and it is important that we make wise ones. If we do, we can shorten those letters to ourselves-at-seventy. We won't have to ask so many questions, because we will know the answers. And that will be just as well, because if we are the kind of people at seventy that we can make ourselves into, we will be far too busy to answer a lot of foolish questions.

IV

The Forgotten Fourth

ONCE UPON A TIME (which is the fairy-tale start of what is becoming more like a fairy tale every day) almost every American home had a "spare room." It was seldom called "the spare room" except in retrospect because it was always occupied. It was known as "Grandma's room" or "Grandpa's room" or "Aunt Mary's room." Some elderly relative lived there as an accepted and beloved member of the immediate family.

I remember "Grandpa's room" in our house for many things, all of them happy. It was a big comfortable room on the second floor that was filled with sunshine and the smell of peppermint. Fat striped peppermint candies to delight exploring little fingers were hidden everywhere: behind pictures, under pillows, and of course in Grandpa's pockets. There were always stories to be listened to and confidences to be exchanged in Grandpa's room.

Most exciting, perhaps, were the secrets we shared, particularly that of the "hangman's rope." Coiled on one of the window-seat cushions, Grandpa kept a stout piece of rope, one end of which was knotted into what looked like a noose. When our mother or any other grownup asked about it, Grandpa's stock reply was "Give a man enough rope, you know . . . ," and he would insist that it be left just where it was.

But we children knew its secret and had a hard time keeping straight faces if we were in the room when he was being questioned. The windows of Grandpa's room looked out upon the sloping porch roof which ran across the front and around one side of the house. An immense old cherry tree grew at the side, its lower branches much too high for us to reach and its trunk too big around and too slippery to afford the arm and toe holds that made it possible for us to climb the other trees. Instead, it laid its tantalizing treasure of juicy, red-black cherries on the porch roof, just out of reach of Grandpa's windows. The porch roof was steep but the noose on the rope made it safe. We would take turns slipping the noose around our waists and clambering out the window, while Grandpa sat on the window seat with a firm grip on the rope. We'd stuff ourselves with cherries until two pulls on the rope signaled that it was time to give the next brother or sister a chance at the bounty. But woe to the child whose school marks were not up to snuff—the two-pull signal would come for him when he had barely got his first taste.

Grandpa came to live with us after Grandma died. They were both in their seventies, and lived in a city a hundred miles from us. It was the most natural thing in the world for him to come to us when he was left alone. And it was the most natural thing in the world for us to open our home to him, not only because he was ours and we were his, but because homes in those days were built to accommodate three generations.

But there are no more comfortable, hospitable, three-generation homes, especially in our cities. The "spare room" has gone out with the antimacassar and the gas light, victim not of changing fashion but of mounting property values, taxes and rentals. Houses are smaller, apartments are shrinking, children are stacked up the walls in double-layer bunk beds, and overnight guests are given the emergency treatment on the living-room sofa. We do not have room any more for our old people, though they may have spent the better part of their working lives sheltering and providing for us.

Yet they are ours, and we are theirs. In their day, in addition to providing for us, they lived the Fourth Commandment which we have forgotten: *Honor thy father and thy mother.* When medical and welfare authorities point out that the care of old people is a direct and personal family responsibility, they are not being original: God said it first, and firmly.

If we ourselves live the "forgotten Fourth," our own children will absorb it as readily and easily as they do the other Commandments in their catechism, and will practice it when our time comes, remembering the love and respect and care we give Grandpa and Grandma now.

When we reach our middle years, we pride ourselves upon being realistic, just as in our younger years we knew ourselves to be idealistic. But we are not so realistic as we think, particularly when it comes to our relationship with our aging parents. It is not entirely our fault, I think, that we confuse legend with living reality. It is because of the temper of the times and the brash youth of our country, so recently sprung from virgin soil, that our thinking has not kept pace with our doing.

Our own grandparents, or their parents, lived on the land. It may have been a farm newly carved out of some pleasant American countryside, or one in Europe handed down through family generations. Ireland is full of such farms, as is the rest of Europe, some of them still being worked by those who remained in the old country, some of them deserted these many years by our parents or grandparents who set sail, on a long-ago morning of heartbreak lightened by hope, to seek opportunity in a vigorous young country beyond the sea.

Many of those who left old-country farms settled in our cities where employment opportunities beckoned, and set their hands to the task of building our industries and our railroads. But their hands remembered the feel of the plow, their nostrils the smell of earth warmed by the sun, their eyes the straight furrows and the tender green first growing, and their hearts the God-given land on which a man might hold up his head and raise his family in a security unshaken by the good and bad turns of the seasons, immovable as the boulders around which he plowed. These things have been bred into us, far below the level of our consciousness.

Some of us remember the land, though we would no longer be content to live on it. Our childhood memories are brightened with the joys of Grandpa's farm, or of Grandma's house in the country. There was substance there, and security, which we needed to taste from time to time for reassurance. We'd spend our vacations there, as we grew older, and take our children for visits that were highlights of their days.

I cannot help wondering what our children think today as they sing the familiar refrain "Over the hills and through the woods to Grandmother's house we go." Has it any meaning to them when they know perfectly well that Grandmother lives in their dining alcove which has been converted into a room by one of those folding accordion doors, or that she lives in a little room a couple of blocks away and goes to business every day, or that she is in that big brick building that smells funny inside where they go visiting every Sunday? There must seem to be two people to them, one the grandmother of unexciting reality, and the other the grandmother of American legend who spends her days baking apple pies and cookies in a rambling vine-covered house set far away among fields and trees and brooks, where tradition beckons us every Thanksgiving to a groaning table, and which is the forgotten source of our popular slogan "home for Christmas."

We are not too different from our children in confusing legend with life; our subconscious often surrounds the old people we know with the old people of legend. And because our old people can no longer live up to the legend, a resentment is bred and festers somewhere deep within us. Parents, according to the legend, are people who represent security, to whom we can turn in need, to whom we can go and with whom we can live as carefree children again when our own adult problems mount and we want to escape them. That there is no longer a basis in fact for such a legend, and that our parents should need our help, is an upset that disturbs us—though we are often unaware, and certainly unwilling to admit, how deeply we are disturbed.

The whole temper of our times is that youth must be served. We admit our responsibility for our children, sacrifice for them, and are determined that they have advantages that we ourselves did not have. We see responsibility as a stream that flows downward, and so cannot conceive of our responsibility flowing upstream to our parents, but accept as natural and normal that their responsibility keep flowing down to us, as ours does to our children. We recognize the fact that physical infirmities or financial circumstances may clog the stream so that as a practical matter their responsibility to us cannot be exercised. But we still feel the downward trend of responsibility the normal one, and our upstream efforts to aid them a sometimes necessary but abnormal state of affairs.

Yet it is significant, I think, that not one of the Commandments is concerned with the care of children. We know, of course, how important children are in the sight of God. We know how Christ loves them, that He commanded us to bring them to Him, that His greatest punishment is reserved for those who scandalize His little ones, and that we ourselves must become as little children in order to enter Heaven. The care of the young is written into the natural law, being rooted so deeply into the instincts of humans and animals alike that we consider the few instances of human mothers or of animals who abandon their young as freaks of nature.

Having already commanded us to care for our children by inscribing the natural law on the fibers of our being, God reserved His Commandments for those explicit commands and prohibitions we need as social beings in order to save our souls. His first three Commandments deal with our responsibilities to Him. The last six take up our responsibilities to society. The Fourth Commandment, *Honor thy father and thy mother,* is placed immediately after our responsibilities to God and before those we owe to society.

The Book of Ecclesiasticus spells it out for us:

"Son, support the old age of thy father, and grieve him not in his life. And if his understanding fail, have patience with him, and despise him not when thou art in thy strength; for the relieving of the father shall not be forgotten. . . . Of what an evil fame is he that forsaketh his father; and he is cursed of God that angereth his mother. . . . Honour thy father, and forget not the groanings of thy mother . . . remember that thou hadst not been born but through them; and make a return to them as they have done for thee."

When I think back to "Grandpa's room," I wonder if I shall ever be the gentle lace-capped inhabitant of "Grandma's room" in one of my sons' homes. It is a sentimental picture that bears little resemblance to reality. I doubt that I shall ever be gentle, though I should like to be, and keep trying to soften my sharp tongue and sweeten the busy efficiency of my days with minutes of fun that accomplish nothing but laughter. And I am certain that I shall never wear a lace cap, nor look in the least like Whistler's mother, because I am not the type.

An old lady I know once voiced a mild complaint, although she knew she was loved and welcomed by the daughter with whom she made her home and by her other children who begged her to share part of each year with them.

"I feel that I'm letting them down," she said. "I'm just not the kind of old mother you see in the movies. I'm just *me*. I'm the same person I've always been. I've worked all my life, and was always more at home over a typewriter than a stove. Why should age suddenly turn me into the priceless cook and home-maker that mothers are supposed to be? I've spent a lifetime writing, so why should I now be thought able to turn out a perfect apple pie? And I've always prided myself on being smartly dressed, so why should I now be expected to show a preference for lavender and old lace?"

Another woman I know is well past her seventieth birthday, although she looks as if she is in her fifties. She lives with her married daughter down the block from me, and passes my house every day on her way to work. Slim and trim, she walks briskly along to the subway like a picture out of the fashion magazines—saucy little hat, smart suit, immaculate gloves, a fresh flower at throat or wrist or pinned for fun on her handbag. She wears glasses, but their tip-tilted frames are the pert harlequin type that young people prefer. I would never believe her age myself, except that I know how many years ago it was that she had to leave her long-time bank job because of the compulsory retirement age of sixty-five. She immediately looked for, and got, another job with no such rule.

Only in the past few years has she eased up a bit, and that not for herself but for the family's convenience. Her daughter felt it necessary to add to the family income by taking a part-time job. The mother too took a part-time job. Now the mother stays home mornings, gets the children off to school, and has lunch ready for them at noon. When they go back to school, she is off to work for the afternoon, and her daughter arrives home from her morning job, having done the marketing on her way. The daughter does the housework, is with the children after school, gets dinner, and greets her husband and mother when they return from work ready for a happy evening when they can all share experiences and interests. It is such a well-adjusted family that I sometimes suspect that the extra income was not important enough to send the daughter off to work, but that she took a part-time job in order to provide a graceful way for her mother to taper off, without however depriving her of a sense of accomplishment and the stimulation of outside contacts.

When I wonder about occupying "Grandma's room" some day, I find myself hoping that I won't. This is not because I do not love my sons, nor is it because I have the slightest doubt of their love or the genuine warmth with which they would welcome me into their families. I hope they will have room for me, but I hope it will be a guest room instead of "my" room, and that I shall be free to come and go as a welcome guest. I hope I will have a home base of my own, even if it is only a tiny room around the corner with a gas plate big enough to hold a pot of coffee. I'd rather have a place where I can leave my quirks and foibles behind when I go visiting than move them permanently into someone's home.

When I am old, I hope my children's love will lead them to plan with me instead of for me. Too many of us, in the rush of sympathy when a parent dies, insist that the survivor live with us. We are especially apt to insist when we have room, but even when it means some inconvenience and crowding we press the matter, not wanting to think of "poor mother" or "poor father" all alone. Poor mother or poor father, in the first daze of bereavement, is apt to consent, and not feel until later the shock of being uprooted from familiar surroundings. Bereavement is easier to bear where roots are deep, and surroundings are filled with memories, and one's accustomed way of life goes on. That way of life may change in some of its aspects, but there is a comforting continuity and familiarity about it. It has not been snapped off, and a new way of life substituted, however well intentioned the snapping off and however pleasant the new way is made.

When one parent dies, we should surround the survivor with evidences of our love and helpfulness, but suggest no changes until the first shock is passed. Then we should discuss with him what *he* wants to do, and make every effort to find ways and means of helping him to do it.

This is what God means by honoring our father and our mother, by respecting their wishes rather than imposing our own. And this is what doctors and welfare experts mean when they say that we should keep old people at home rather than institutionalize them. Home is the natural place for the old, as it is for children. By "home" they mean, first of all, the old person's own home, and only when that is impossible, the home of a child or other relative. The primary medicine for old people is the maintaining of their independence and consequent self-respect.

Of course it is not always possible for an old person to be independent and live alone. Physical infirmities or mental disorders, not severe enough to require hospitalization, may make it necessary for him to live within a family where watchfulness and care and companionship are constantly available. Sometimes, too, old people genuinely prefer to live with their children—a widowed man, particularly, who has been catered to by a loving wife through the years and who is helpless when she goes, never having learned how to cook or clean house or even keep his clothes in order.

God tells us to respect their wishes, and the welfare experts tell us to encourage their independence. These are not contradictories, because even when an old person expresses a wish to live with us, his more fundamental wish is to retain his independence. Therefore we should first explore the possibilities of his living apart from us, with our loving support and encouragement.

Is it possible for the surviving parent to keep on living in the family home? I know of many who are doing so, though at first thought it did not seem possible.

One man has an apartment in the city. He has no financial difficulties, but it is not easy for him to get about, and he has no knowledge whatever of cooking or other household skills. He is fiercely independent, however, and when his wife died he turned down his children's entreaties to live with them. "I'll make out," he told them, and went on to show them how.

He advertised in the newspapers, and after some careful screening he selected a young couple to whom he offered rent-free one of his bedrooms, the use of the living room and kitchen privileges in return for the wife's keeping the apartment tidy and cooking his simple meals. It has turned out to be a happy arrangement, and they are good friends. The saving of rent has proved a godsend to the husband, a struggling young junior executive, and instead of cooking separately for the old man the couple insists that he share their meals, which he does with great enjoyment.

Another man was left alone in a comfortable house not far from one of New York's city colleges. It was difficult for him to maintain it alone, both physically and financially. He worked out a plan whereby he has managed to fill his home with teachers from the college who enjoy the convenience of living so near by. Since they are all teachers the house has taken on the atmosphere of a club, and the old man enjoys sitting in occasionally on the discussions. The income he receives, in addition to providing for his own modest needs, makes it possible for him to hire a woman to clean house and prepare his meals as well as breakfast for his roomers, and a part-time handyman to take care of the maintenance and heavy work.

There is a woman I know who has never worked outside her home and who had no training or skills that she knew of that could be turned into income-producers. But she had always been a wonderful home-maker. It was that art that enabled her to maintain her home, and continue to live comfortably where her roots were deep. She had no trouble renting out rooms and keeping her guests happy with her gracious hospitality.

There is an unusual restaurant in New York, owned and operated by much the same kind of woman. She has a beautiful home, and its furnishings make it obvious that at one time she and her husband had a great deal of money and lived well. But through the years after his death she had to cut into their savings, and huge taxes on such a large piece of property in the heart of the city pretty nearly wiped them out. She did not relish the idea of roomers, but wanted to keep her home. Though in the past she had had servants, she herself had always been an excellent cook, and thus her unique restaurant idea was born.

She decided to serve dinner each evening to the public, just as she had so often served it to her own guests. There is no indication on the outside of the house that it is anything but a fine private home, and she uses no advertising except word-of-mouth publicity from those who know of her project. You must telephone a few days ahead to make a reservation for dinner, since she limits the number of guests to twenty—all her beautiful dining room can seat comfortably.

You arrive at the appointed time and ring the bell. A trim maid greets you and your dinner companion at the door, takes your coats, and ushers you into the living room where a fire is crackling on the hearth—or, if it is summer, the long windows are open upon the garden. Your hostess, dressed for dinner, welcomes you and introduces you to the other guests who have arrived. There is pleasant conversation over a cocktail or sherry for half an hour, and then a gracious procession to the dining room.

You note the mahogany furniture gleaming deep with the loving polishing of years, the fine silver and crystal and linen, the fresh flowers and the soft glow of candlelight from the clusters of tall candles in their silver holders. You and the others gather around the table and then, surprisingly, the hostess unaffectedly says grace. It is the perfect start to a perfect meal.

The service is family style with second helpings urged. The food is fabulous, and the meal is expensive but well worth it judging by the fact that there is never an empty chair at the table. The woman does the cooking and supervising herself, manages with a minimum of help, works afternoons only, and makes a very comfortable living. She seems to look younger each year, because she is independent, doing work she enjoys, providing good food for a constant succession of friendly people, and the future of her home is assured.

There are many ways in which, with planning and encouragement, it is possible to prevent the uprooting of an old person from the home which has been his through the years.

On the other hand, if it does not seem wise to continue living in the family home, if it is too big to manage or if it is too inconveniently located for an old person who has been left alone and who finds that distances increase interminably with age, independent living can still be planned and made possible in a smaller place that is nearer to family and friends, to church and shopping, recreation and transportation.

Planning with instead of for our old people is not only being obedient to the Fourth Commandment, but is living the Golden Rule. If we measure our middle years by the Golden Rule and do to others as we would have them do to us, we shall find our own later years lightened and brightened by that same Rule.

V

The Formula

LIVING ALONE in our later years need have nothing to do with loneliness, but can have much to do with independence. Both are spiritual qualities—the one a disease that withers and kills, the other a tonic that strengthens the spirit and helps it grow.

Perhaps, since this is a thinking-aloud, I should confess to a sense of absurdity in speaking of "independence" and letting the word stand alone, because the longer I live the more I realize how dependent each one of us is. We are utterly dependent, each instant of our lives, upon God Who willed us into being, and sustains us in existence, and without Whose continuing act of will we should immediately return to the nothingness from which He created us. We are dependent upon all of His creatures, and most particularly upon those who share His life with us and share, too, the responsibility of lighting the world with His truth and warming it with His love.

We are created to be social beings, so that no one of us can live to ourselves, independently of others, even if we should wish to. Independence of this sort does violence to our human nature and destroys it, because it is a perversion of freedom.

We are free, and yet we are dependent. Being such de-

pendent creatures—upon God, upon our family and friends,
upon the work which earns our livelihood and the employer
who pays us for it, upon strangers who provide and transport and sell our necessities to us, upon doctors and teachers and farmers and writers and bus drivers and policemen
and firemen and a thousand others—in what sense should
we strive to be independent the day after tomorrow?

It is in this important sense: that we carry our own burdens, and if possible help others to carry theirs, and that we
do not ourselves become a burden upon them. The importance of independence to us lies solely in its value to
others. The wrong kind of independence is a self-sufficiency,
the right kind is a self-giving.

There is a somewhat inelegant expression that describes
women, particularly talkative busybodies like me, as "old
bags." That's what my best friend and severest critic sometimes calls me. "The wonders of modern science never fail
to amaze me," he will say, when I return from a trip to the
beauty parlor. "Here I had breakfast this morning with an
old bag, and I'm dining with a glamor-puss."

He doesn't believe I'm an old bag yet, any more than I
believe that I am, or ever could be, a glamor-puss. But some
day I'm going to be an old bag, and when that day comes I
hope I'll be an independent one. Because an independent
bag can be useful to people—it can carry provisions for
them, and store their secrets safely, be rolled into a pillow
to ease their sleep or torn into strips to bind their hurts,
warm them by being tucked into drafty window frames, and
amuse their children in a hundred games. But the same bag
can be a burden for a man and his family to keep carrying, when it is filled with infirmity and anxiety and irritation
and complaints.

It may be that God is planning to fill the bag of my years
with infirmities and poverty and strap me to someone's back.

If that is to be His way of cutting me to size for Heaven, I shall be grateful to Him, and try to lie as lightly and comfortably as possible upon the generous back to which I have been strapped. I shall know that what He is doing is good for me and good for the owner of the back. But it will be good for neither of us if I become a self-made burden through lack of foresight and preparation.

We can be an independent source of strength and comfort to others whether we live with them or apart from them, but it is easier when we live apart. Old people, with the best of intentions, become fixed in their ways. Habits of a lifetime have dug deep channels by the time the later years are reached, and they are not easily changed.

Parents who have been heads-of-the-house all their married lives, who have been the ones to make decisions, to determine what is to be done and how it should be done, do not take easily to becoming "fifth wheels" in another house where others make the decisions and carry them out in strange and new-fangled ways.

It is particularly difficult for an elderly maiden aunt or bachelor uncle to fit in gracefully; a parent through the years has had a partner and thus has been trained in the arts of cooperation and adjustment and compromise for the sake of family harmony, but a single person has lived a lifetime of being his own boss. He has had to learn cooperation and adjustment in his business and social relations in order to make a living and be accepted, but he has not had to learn them in the deep areas of his personal life where likes and dislikes grow, habits are shaped and personality becomes fixed.

A maiden aunt might sniff indignantly and stalk from the room when nephew lights a cigar, or turn down a proffered dish with, "Sweetbreads? Ugh! Thank you, my dear, but you should know I never touch the stuff."

A mother might sniff at the cigar too, but it would be a nostalgic sniff. "It reminds me of Dad," she might say. "How he loved a good cigar, especially after dinner. I can see him now." And as for the sweetbreads . . . "No, I never could get to like them, but Dad did. Here, let me show you how I used to fix them for him."

Of course maiden aunts and bachelor uncles have advantages too. No one, not even grandparents, are more patient with children, or more generous. There are exceptions, of course, but by and large the single person who has never known the care and responsibility of bringing up children discovers each facet of their development with fresh delight and extravagant praise, and is eager to foster the hero worship which his young relatives are ready to lavish upon him.

If we should find ourselves physically or financially dependent upon others some day, and must live with and be provided for by them, we can still be spiritually independent, and make our "bag of years" less of a burden by filling it with charity and a fine Christian dignity.

Our room in the household, however tiny, is ours. We can welcome other members of the family to it, and respect their privacy as we would wish them to respect ours by confining ourselves and our belongings to it as much as possible. There is no dignity without privacy, and privacy works both ways.

"Mother *snoops* so," I heard a distracted wife say. "Oh, she doesn't read my mail or listen in on the phone. But she'll rummage around until she finds what I paid for the meat we had Sunday, and no matter how good a buy I thought it was, she'll grumble all week about how extravagant I am. She picks my friends apart, and the neighbors too—I don't know where she digs it up, but she finds gossip about all of them. Linda can't give a party without Mother parading through the living room a dozen times during the evening, with one excuse or another, just to see what's going on. It's the same thing when Bill and I want to talk about something, or go over the bills, or figure out the income tax. Mother's always right in the next room, with her ears flapping. She even turns off the television, so she won't miss a word."

Like privacy, we should remember that helpfulness too works both ways. True helpfulness is the kind that helps another when he wishes it and in the manner he wishes it. His ideas may differ from ours and to insist upon ours is the opposite of helpfulness.

"The house isn't big enough to hold Uncle John and me," a friend of mine told me, in a rush of confidence that seemed to relieve her. "I blame myself, and I'm so ashamed because really he's a dear, and he tries so hard to help. He insists on making his own breakfast every morning, and he's burned out two of our coffeepots already. He insists on washing the Sunday dishes too—that's his job, he says, and he's so proud of it I can't say a word. I have to wait until after he's in bed at night, and when I'm dead tired, to wash them all over again. He can't see well, and he just doesn't notice egg stains or grease spots. And he thinks he's a handyman. You should see the paint job he did on the porch—it's really funny, but you feel like crying. I wish I could tell him that he'd be more of a help if he wouldn't *try* so hard to help."

A willingness and happy readiness to help with household chores, or minding the children, or any one of the countless ways in which a household needs help, is sufficient. Our pleasure at any task given us, and our conscientious performance of it, prove that our desire to help is genuine, particularly if we are considerate enough to ask if there is any special way in which the person who gave us the task prefers to have it done.

In some ways, one of the most difficult lessons we shall have to learn if we are some day transplanted into a household not our own, is that it is *not* our own. We are no longer in command, and have no right to demand or to criticize, and should give neither advice nor suggestions unless they are asked for. There is no room in a three-generation household for an "I told you so," or "If you had done it *my* way," or "Don't forget that I've had more experience than you."

We learn through mistakes, and the experience we are so proud of is built on them. We may think we know better ways of doing things, but we may be wrong.

Who am I to explain to a daughter-in-law some day that turkey requires long cooking in a slow oven, when her new electronic range may be able to baste it to a turn in ten minutes? Even today I see my young daughter-in-law feeding her baby "on demand" with the approval of the baby's doctor, and remember only ten brief years ago when my youngest son was born, how I was supposed to let him howl rather than shorten his strict four-hour feeding schedule by as little as a few minutes. We live, but many of us do not learn. Both processes should go hand in hand through the years.

An important way in which we can be helpful in any household is to keep our love and interest steadfastly focused on the other members, and resolutely turned away from ourselves. We must keep reminding ourselves that we are not in that household simply to receive, but more importantly to give. We have been placed there not by the accidents of need and circumstance, because there are no accidents with God, but rather because of the needs and circumstances of the household itself. God places us there purposefully in order that we supply something that household needs. It may be true that we ourselves have needs that we depend upon the household to supply. But it is also true that God gave us needs of that particular nature in order that we make our home where we ourselves are needed. He could have given us other needs or met our needs in other ways.

Whether or not we are able to help with household chores, baby-sitting, the children's homework, or in other such ways, the prime needs of every household are ones that we can supply even if we are confined to our beds.

Every household, without exception, needs love and understanding and prayer. Love, though it is the deep bond that unites the household, is too often left unexpressed in the rush of daily affairs. Friction and stress often twist understanding into misunderstanding with consequent hurt. And prayer is all too often perfunctory in the hurried activities, pressures and anxieties of busy days. God places us in the household to supply these needs.

Love needs expression, primarily in actions but also in words. Why have we become so self-conscious and so afraid of sentiment that the words "I love you" embarrass us except when voiced privately between real-life lovers, or blatantly between their movie or TV versions? Why shouldn't it be heard more frequently between parents and their children, even between aged parents and their grown-up children? Why shouldn't it be a simple and truthful and entirely natural expression of deep affection among close friends?

"I love you" is the natural expression of a child, which comes welling out of his simplicity and truth, and we are not embarrassed when we hear him say it. But we consider it to be weakness on the part of an adult, a sign of the lowering or collapsing of his defenses. It is a curious twisting, in an attempt at self-justification, to describe as "defenses" the encrustations of pride and selfishness with which we have blocked the pathway to our spirit. A child has no such "defenses," nor should we, remembering that we must become like children in order to enter Heaven. Our love should be as free-flowing and as naturally expressed as a child's. It was thus in the childhood of the Church, when love was the one characteristic that identified the early Christians to the pagans around them. "See how they love one another," the pagans said.

But to say "I love you" is hollow and a meaningless mockery if we do not live our love and prove it by our actions.

I used to be deeply troubled about God's command that we love our neighbors, by which He means that we are to love everyone. "I just *can't* love everyone," I thought. "Imagine loving that loudmouth at the office who manages to put a dirty double meaning into everything he says. Or the busybody down the block who works so hard tearing everybody's reputation to shreds. Or the show-off who pulled a lot of shady strings to get herself elected president of the club and who now keeps playing favorites."

Much earlier, I had been even more deeply troubled about loving God.

"I *want* to love God," I kept saying to myself, "but I just can't. I don't feel a thing. I can go to Mass, I can think about Him, I can pray, I can do all the things He wants me to do, and I know all the reasons why I should love Him. But I can't manage to feel any love."

It was a good priest who straightened me out.

"Love has nothing to do with feeling," he told me. "Love is a matter of the will. When you want to love God, and when you act as if you love Him, you do indeed love Him. You can't depend on feelings—they are fickle, and can come from many things besides love. When you go to Mass and feel exalted and brimming over with love for God, it may be no more than your mood. Perhaps you're feeling good, and it's a beautiful day, or you're looking forward to some happy activity. You'd be surprised at how many people feel they love God at Easter, especially a sunny, warm Easter when they can show off their new clothes, and the church is full of flowers, and all of spring is ahead after a long winter. Christmas too—so many people feel that they love Him in a rush of sentiment at hearing the familiar Christmas carols and the excitement of giving and opening gifts. But when you pray, even though you don't feel like praying, or go to Mass when you're tired and headachy and it's raining and you haven't a spark of fervor—then you're showing God that you really love Him. You're putting His will before your own inclinations. You're acting *as if* you love Him. And that means you really do."

It took a long time for me to realize that the same thing is true of all the people we are commanded to love, and even longer before I could learn to love the office loudmouth, and the neighborhood busybody, and the club show-off, and a dozen others in this realistic way. I could certainly never muster up any loving feelings toward them, and it was a great relief when I found I didn't have to.

Love, Father said, was a matter of the will, and I could express it by acting toward others *as if* I loved them. It was easy, because I had only to observe how I acted toward those I was conscious of loving deeply, and then try to act the same way to others.

When we love, we put the welfare and interests of those we love above our own. We think of them and pray for them often, enjoy being in their company, rejoice at their good fortune, and try to lighten their misfortunes in any way we can. Since love is a giving, we express it with gifts, especially the giving of ourselves in acts of kindness and thoughtfulness and helpfulness.

We can do the same with those who irritate and repel us most. When in their company we can act *as if* we enjoyed being there. We can act *as if* we rejoiced in their good fortune, by being quick with congratulations or praise or a gift to suit the occasion. We can pray for them, and think of them often, and show them that we do so by keeping in touch with them even though privately we think we would be happy if we never saw them again. We can give of ourselves by going out of our way to be helpful, and by the frequent performance of little uncalled-for acts of kindness and consideration.

Such is the alchemy of love, that merely acting *as if* we love transforms what we do into expressions of actual love. Try it, for a wonderful surprise. For you will find that you cannot act as if you loved someone for any length of time without finding that you actually do love him, and without discovering the joy of your love being returned.

It is God's own formula for love, because He never commands us to do something without at the same time giving us the means of doing it. And it is a most practical formula to take with us into our later years. If we were wiser than we are, we would use it all our lives, and not pick and choose among the acquaintances of our young and middle years and squander the others because it is too much of an effort to try to love them too. But in our later years we may find ourselves living among people not of our own choosing, and it will be a purgatory indeed if we do not love them. If we are unmarried and have never lived in a close and loving relationship with members of the household we find ourselves in, several or all of them may rub us the wrong way, and we may take a perverted kind of pleasure in doing the same to them. Or if we have been married, and are now living in the household of a beloved son, we may find our daughter-in-law a thorn in our aged side, and launch an undeclared war that makes the entire household, and especially ourselves, utterly miserable.

With God's *"as if"* formula we can, as we must, love them all. The old man who claimed not to have had any enemies knew the secret. Those who heard him thought he was boasting outrageously until they asked him how he could have gone through a long lifetime without enemies. "I made friends of them," he said simply.

If, in the divine scheme of things, we some day find ourselves living in and dependent physically or financially upon another household, we must be spiritually independent because we have been placed there to supply that family's need for love that is expressed and demonstrated.

If we put the family's welfare and interests before our own, we shall not magnify nor even mention our own complaints. We shall be the trusted repository of confidences. If we do not offer opinions or advice, we shall be asked for them. We shall be good listeners, something everyone has need for and that few people can find these days when we are all so filled with our own concerns that we have neither time nor inclination to listen to those of others. I think a large part of our confusion today exists because everyone is talking about himself, and a major cause of our frustration is that there is no one to listen.

We are to be the hearth around which all the members of the family gather, because our love is constantly burning there—cheering the eye, comforting the body and warming the heart.

But we are also there to keep the peace. "Blessed are the peacemakers," says Christ. He puts us, infirm as we may be, into the household to bring His peace like a benediction down upon it. We are not to take sides, nor show preferences, but rather to promote understanding, smooth out irritations and soothe injured feelings.

Being a peacemaker would seem to be a full-time job in many busy households today. Son brings his troubles home from the office. Daughter is ready to scream at the children. Junior is in a rage because he can't have the car for the evening. Sis is sulking because she can't stay out late with the crowd. The whole family is up in arms over the question of the curfew, or the children sharing household responsibilities, or where to spend the vacation, or the matter of "going steady." Such a family needs a peacemaker who does not take sides, but who loves both sides so much that each knows the older person has his deepest interests at heart and so is willing to listen.

Yes, it is a full-time job and a difficult one, but its rewards are out of all proportion to the effort. "Blessed are the peacemakers," says Christ, "for they shall be called children of God."

Most of all, God places us in a household in order that we may *pray* for its members. Prayer is the most important contribution we can make to the family, the greatest help we can give them, and the most perfect expression of our love for them. We are to be individual powerhouses of prayer, working full time and with full hearts and minds at praying for those around us who have so little time to pray, and who do that little with troubled hearts and distracted minds.

We will find much time to pray, and much to pray for, during the long quiet years ahead. We can pray for each member of the family, knowing his needs and being able to present them to God from the close vantage point of His vestibule. Our prayers have such a short distance to go in those years, that we can be sure they will be heard.

Daily Mass is often impossible in a busy household, with Father rushing to the office and Mother rushing to get the youngsters off to school. But we, if we are physically able, can take the family's troubles to Mass with us each morning and leave them at the altar, and bring back God's blessing upon the family's day.

We can do more than pray for the family's needs. We can offer God the praise and adoration and love that they are often too busy to give Him, and thank Him for the blessings that they too often accept thoughtlessly. And we can do even more. We can offer up our aches and pains, our infirmities and discomforts for the family. When we pray for a troubled or erring member of the family, for a sick person or for one who has strayed from the Faith, we can be sure God hears. But when we offer Him, at the same time, our blindness or lameness or sleepless nights, the stroke which has paralyzed us or the arthritis which has crippled us or the cancer which ravages us, God will not be outdone in generosity.

Perhaps we can be the ones to start family prayer, or the family Rosary, if these have not already become established customs. Father Peyton's "The family that prays together, stays together" has become so familiar a slogan that we are tempted to think of it as no more than a slogan, and so are apt to be surprised all over again when we see how surely it works out. If it seems difficult to start such a custom, we can begin with the children, gathering them around us for prayers at bedtime. It will not be long before the family joins in.

We can above all share the joys of God's vestibule with the children. They will understand and respond, because they are so fresh from there themselves. Perhaps that is why youngsters and old people are so close to one another. Have you wondered why they are not strangers? It is because they have met before, in God's vestibule: the little ones coming out, and the old ones coming back.

We can read to the children and have them read to us, using books about God and His saints and His Church that are appropriate to their age level. We can hear their catechism lessons and make them come alive with stories. We can talk to them about God and our Blessed Mother and the saints as familiarly as if they were people in the next room, which in truth they are.

We will be stepping into the next room ourselves before long, and we shall certainly want to leave the door open so the family can join us, and a light burning so they can find their way.

VI

Declaration of Independence

I<small>F WE</small> have done all we can to enable us in our later years to live independently and apart from the family so that we will not be a burden to them, and if despite our efforts we find that we must live with them, we can be sure that God has taken the matter out of our hands and placed us there because we are needed there. He has a job for us that no one else can do, and we should accept it with gratitude and perform it with joy.

But it is still our responsibility to lay the groundwork for a declaration of independence in later years, by way of planning and preparation during our middle years. Our planning must include personal programs designed to maintain our health and furnish us with some measure of financial independence during the years when self-support largely ceases. Only when we have done that can we plan independent living for ourselves on the assumption that, God willing, we shall be physically and financially able to live independently.

There is no single plan that will fit all old people. In fact, I doubt that there is any single plan that will fit, in every detail, more than a single old person. Because old people, like the rest of us, are individuals; each has his abilities, habits, likes and dislikes. They share only the weight of years and the desire for independence.

My idea of living alone in a small place (small enough to care for easily but big enough to put up an overnight guest or two) across the street from church, around the corner from the family, a short walking distance from friends and doctor, shops and transportation may attract some people and repel others.

Many people look forward to the years after retirement as the time when they can do all the traveling they could not do while they were tied down by household cares or business responsibilities. They would like some day to see as much of the country or of the world as they can, freed of time schedules and the necessity of being home by a given date. I know one such person who declared that his retirement home will be wherever he finds himself—he plans to invest in a trailer.

Other people would like to strike new roots in some part of the country at a distance from where they have always lived, and the problem is deciding where to settle. Many of them are attracted by a warmer climate, and think longingly of Florida or Southern California or the Southwest. Two unmarried sisters who have taught school all their lives, and whose retirement is approaching, told me that their idea of Heaven is a place where it's always warm and sunny and where there are "no more frozen water pipes, no more snow shoveling, no more trying to start a balky car on a bitter morning."

Others who feel that they will be able to stay in their present homes are wondering if they should stay there or should instead plan a retirement home of a size and in a location more in keeping with their future abilities and interests. Still others are attracted by the possibilities of group living, either in one of the many communities that are being built with the needs of old people in mind, or in a home for the aged.

Whatever your own preferences it is wise to remember that wishful thinking accomplishes nothing, and that only realistic planning now leads to rewarding results later. There are many possibilities, and many ways to plan where and how we shall live when we are old. It is important to investigate the advantages and disadvantages of each, and evaluate these in terms of our own personalities and abilities so that our plans will be practical and give at least some promise of success.

We must know ourselves before we can plan for ourselves. As we go through our middle years many of our friends retire, and we are sometimes tempted to make the mistake of planning for ourselves the kind of life they have chosen, after hearing their enthusiastic reports.

Our neighbors the Smiths have settled happily in a Florida resort town, and may be urging us to join them. We may turn green with envy when the morning mail brings us postcards from the footloose Joneses who are traveling over the face of the earth, staying wherever they like for as long as they like. We may exclaim over the snug retirement home, with its many labor-saving conveniences, which the Browns have built for themselves out in the country. Or we may drop in to visit Mr. and Mrs. Green in a nearby home for the aged and have all our notions about such homes changed as we see how much like a fine hotel it is and how happy the Greens are in their attractive room surrounded by their treasured possessions.

"This," we may say, "is for us."

Which is really for us? That depends upon the kind of people we are.

Living independently, of course, need not mean living entirely alone. Do we enjoy being alone or do we need con-

stant companionship? Would we be happy living by ourselves and being able to visit other people or have them
visit us at times of our own choosing? Would we be happier
living with someone in order to share companionship and
expenses? Do we like having lots of people around us; do we
find them enjoyable and interesting or do they tire us? Are
we individualists or would we fit gracefully into group living, finding that its conveniences outweigh its restrictions?

Can we keep ourselves interested and contented? Do we
enjoy doing those things which we can do by ourselves anywhere: reading, listening to the radio or watching television,
busying ourselves with handiwork or hobbies, puttering
about the house or workshop or garden? Or do the things
we enjoy doing mean that we shall have to be near places
where we can do such things as fishing or hunting or taking
adult education courses, or being with people who can share
our pleasure at golfing, auctions, playing bingo or canasta,
participating in discussion groups or club activities?

Have we always welcomed the excitement and challenge
of change: new places, new friends, new experiences? Or do
we enjoy the comfort and security of familiar places and
faces? Have we always been active and on the go? Or have
we been sedentary? Much as we may have liked to travel,
have we always felt "it's good to be home again?" Have we
moved frequently, whether by choice or necessity? If so,
have we enjoyed pulling up stakes and starting fresh or has
the adjustment been difficult?

Are we gregarious, warm, outgoing, the kind of people
who make friends easily? Or are we more reserved, and
find that it takes us a while to become acquainted in a new
place?

Answers to questions such as these will help to pinpoint
the location and type of life we should plan. They will
help take our measurements so that we may custom-tailor

our later years to fit us comfortably. But we must remember that we are measuring with a future yardstick and make allowances for shrinkage.

Our zest for traveling about, our pleasure in new scenes and new people, our eagerness to pull up stakes and go seeking adventure may diminish considerably when the weight of our years lies heavy upon us. However much we may enjoy active sports now, we may find that a spectator role fits us better later on. Our present home, or the one we dream of having, may be set high on a hill with a thrilling view or be tucked away far back from the road for privacy. But that hill may some day become insurmountable or the distance from that road interminable, when the years slow us down and stretch even short spans into hardship.

The urge to travel, in the years ahead when we are free to do so, is an urge that is shared by many people, and I am one of them. I should like to travel the length and breadth of this country, seeing our future in its expanding cities and our past in all the places where history has been written in victory and defeat and valor. I should like to go poking into little towns and hamlets and detouring through back roads, stopping off here and there—almost everywhere —to savor the full flavor of America. I should like to be able to spend enough time in Italy and France and England, and all over Europe to season the discoveries of return trips with the sweet taste of the familiar. I should like to live a while, quietly and alone, in Bethlehem and in Nazareth and walk the roads of Galilee and climb the Mount of Olives. I should like to follow in the footsteps of St. Paul as he journeyed from Jerusalem to Rome.

Yet such travels will in no way lessen my need for the little-room-around-the-corner, which my mind is furnishing even now with a coffeepot and a typewriter and the most beautiful statue of Our Lady that I can find. That little room will become more necessary than ever if I travel, because a traveler needs roots.

Travel is a purposeful journeying. It need have no time limits but it must have a point of departure, a destination or objective and a point of return if it is to be enriching, enjoyable and meaningful. Without a home base travel becomes a wandering, and a traveler without home roots a sort of vagabond. In song and story vagabonds are supposed to be carefree, happy people, but in real life they are people who have lost their way despite their intimate knowledge of train and plane and ship schedules—they are restless, rootless, haunted by the feeling of not "belonging" anywhere, urged on by an insecurity they will not admit to the everlasting quest of a security they profess not to want.

If you have always longed to travel, whether to discover new places or to revisit those of happy memory, by all means plan to go if you can. But when you do be sure that you have a home from which you can set out and which will welcome you when you return. Plan to be away as frequently and as long as your inclinations and strength and finances will allow, but remember that you experience only a third of the joy of travel en route. The first third is anticipation, planning your trip within your own four walls. And the last third, which can last you the rest of your life, is reliving your travels when you are back home again.

I know a couple who built a travel fund of dollars and dreams through the years when the husband was tied to his office and the wife to their home and children. Their dreams were given substance, and their future traveling made more enjoyable, by reading and learning as much as they could about all the places they wanted to visit. The first thing they did after the husband retired was to make a "grand tour" around the world. It was lengthy and expensive, but well worth-while because it has enriched their lives ever since. If they never again leave the town where they live, they are satisfied. They have seen the rest of the world and have enjoyed it, and their enjoyment cannot be taken from them.

The adventures of another old couple were reported in the newspapers recently. According to the accounts, they took their life savings of about $20,000 and traveled through Europe until the money was spent. Apparently they figured a little too closely, because I remember reading that they had to spend a while in a London poorhouse until arrangements could be made to get them home. What they are doing now, I do not know. They have their memories but, popular sentiment to the contrary, memories are not too satisfactory substitutes for food and clothing and shelter. The spirit of adventure must be tempered by prudence.

And then there was Bridie, the old Irish cook who inspired so many and scandalized so many more by the use to which she put her travel dollars. "Bridie's fund" was well known in the community where I grew up. We all knew her well, because she had cooked for so many of us over the years. We knew her as a devoted friend and a dedicated worker who had but two wishes: to visit Rome and to get to Ireland in time to die. She gave generously of her wages to her parish church, spent practically nothing on herself, and put the rest into "Bridie's fund" to realize her dream. When the time finally came and she was ready to retire, we rejoiced with her that the fund was so substantial. She came around to each of our houses to say good-by, with her funny little hat perched on the back of her head and her big worn handbag swinging from her arm by its stout strap. We eyed the handbag, begged her to be careful of her money and wished her godspeed.

Two days later she was back asking for work again, saying that she had "changed her mind" about the trip. We were alarmed because her money was gone and questioned her closely. But Bridie kept her own counsel. She would not tell us what had happened to her money, but she was not worried. She was obviously happy as she went about her work. Only when we threatened to report the matter to the authorities for her own good did she tell us the story. It was a short one, and simple.

"Bridie O'Brien," she had said to herself, "it is to Heaven you should be going. Aren't you the foolish one, taking such a long way around? There is a shorter way, and surer."

So she had marched into the Chancery Office, and turned her travel money into a fund to educate priests. How many young men since that time have felt "Bridie's fund" like a comforting and supporting arm around their shoulders, helping them on their long climb to the altar, only God knows—and Bridie, who has been with Him these past many years.

Lack of roots at a time when he will need them is what disturbs me about the man who told me that he plans to have a trailer as his retirement home. However, it may be only my personal disinclination to trailer life that influences my thinking. Certainly there are thousands of people, including whole families, who find trailer life exciting and enjoyable, and trailer parks and facilities are found all over the country in answer to the demand. These people like the freedom and change of a mobile way of living, and if you have similar tastes you will find many to share them.

However, it is wise to try out this kind of life before you settle for it. Trailers are expensive, ranging from one to many thousand dollars, depending upon their size and equipment. Before giving up your home and investing in a trailer, plan to rent one and spend a month or two seeing how you like the life of a trailerite. If you don't, you will have lost little more than the price of a vacation trip. If you do, you will probably be allowed to apply what you have already paid in rental toward the purchase price of the trailer. But several enthusiastic trailer owners I know have their cake and eat it too: they have kept their homes, and use their trailers for vacations in summer and trips south in winter. Even the most enthusiastic of them confesses to having a "good to be home" feeling when he and his wife round the corner after a trip to distant parts and see their house waiting for them.

Roots sustain life. Seedlings are meant to be transplanted from the warm nursery where they were sheltered to the open soil where they send forth eager roots. Almost any plant, when it is young and vigorous, can be transplanted to new ground and will readily push down roots and grow. But the older the plant, the slower its growth, and the greater the danger of transplanting. Old roots take their life-giving nourishment most easily from familiar soil. They seldom survive for long the shock of uprooting and replanting in a strange soil and climate. We are much the same.

We must be on guard, therefore, to act thoughtfully rather than impulsively in the first flush of freedom we feel as our later years loosen the ties and responsibilities that have long restricted our activities to a limited area. When the time comes, we city-bound people who have been dreaming of the quiet joys of country life may be tempted to act too hastily. When we settle down in the country we may find those "quiet joys" much over-rated. The quiet may be far too quiet for our city-bred ears, and the distances too great. We may miss the city's conveniences which we had always taken for granted, and the rush and noise and crowds and "aliveness" of the city which we were in such a hurry to escape.

Country-bred people who have always dreamed of the excitement of the city may find loneliness in the midst of the crowds. A city can be cold to those who were not raised on its pavements and shaped to its pattern during their formative years. People can become lost in a city, and its crowds are too busy to care. It is not that city people are unkind, but simply that they are preoccupied, and there are so many strangers among their own that they cannot recognize a stranger from outside who needs the comfort of neighborliness.

In the country or in a small town we know almost everybody, at least by sight. City people move, day and night, among strange faces, and are at home in the anonymity of a crowd. They must seek out their friends, because they are seldom close neighbors. City apartment dwellers often do not know the families who live alongside in the same apartment house.

If our dream has always been to move from city to country, or vice versa, we should start during our young adult years sending down tentative exploratory roots in one or the other. We can spend our vacations in city or country, trying as much as possible to live as "natives" rather than as vacationers. Whether our vacation lasts two weeks or a month or more, we should shun city hotels and find a furnished room or rent an apartment, and pass up resort hotels, country inns and boardinghouses in favor of renting a place of our own —a house, a cabin or a room or two in someone's home. Only when we live "on our own" can we experience any taste of what life would be like for us should we some day decide to settle there and share that life with the natives. We must come to know its inconveniences as intimately as we do its conveniences, and look below its tourist attractions for those things that attract and hold its residents. When we do our own shopping and cooking and laundry, and rely upon the local stores and doctors and dentists for our necessities, upon local facilities for our recreation and interests, upon local people for our companionship, we will have a sounder basis for evaluation.

During our young adult years, with many a vacation ahead of us, we can afford to put down such exploratory roots in a number of different localities so that actual experience will guide us when it is time to make a choice. We must be careful, however, not to make all our vacations summer ones. We must come to know the localities that interest us in all their seasons. One that is beautiful and invigorating during the summer may be snowed-in or rainy and bleak during the winter. One that is balmy during the winter may be fiercely hot during the summer. One that boasts of its climate both summer and winter may be subject at other times to floods, hurricanes or dust storms. A resort town that is lively with people and activities during the season may close down to a hush and be all but deserted during the off-season.

During our middle years our preparation should be more purposeful. These are the years during which we should buy or build our retirement home, so that it will be ready when we are. Our previous years of exploration should have narrowed our choice to one or a few localities, if they have not determined us to stay where our roots have been growing through the years.

Suppose you have decided upon a place where you think you can settle down happily for the rest of your life, once the time has come for settling down. Suppose that your visits and vacations there at different seasons of the year have left you with a liking for the people and the climate and the facilities. It is time, then, to investigate other important factors.

If you plan to live on your retirement income, or on your savings, are you sure you will have enough to support yourself in that locality? If you must supplement what income you will have with a job, or rely entirely upon a job, what employment opportunities does the locality offer? Is such employment seasonal or steady? What are the prevailing wages in the area? And what are the local prices for food and goods and services?

Authorities warn against pulling up stakes and moving to a new locality before first visiting it and thoroughly exploring its opportunities. They advise putting your problem, your job requirements if any, your retirement status, and all pertinent facts and questions into a letter to the Chamber of Commerce in the area where you are thinking of living. In addition they urge that you buy copies of the local newspapers of the area at your out-of-town newsstand, or subscribe directly to them, and read them as carefully as if you were a local resident concerned with all that is going on.

You may be sure that all local problems will be thoroughly aired in such newspapers, and as you follow them you will be able to get the feel and flavor and "temper" of the place. You will begin to distinguish the local forces working for the good of the community from those obstructing its progress and, before long, the individuals responsible for one or the other. You will see what recreational facilities are available, and how the community supports its churches, schools, libraries, hospitals and programs for civic and social betterment.

But read on. Where is your church located? Is it nearby, or will you have to travel to the next town for Mass and parish activities? Is there a doctor and a dentist in town? An oculist, a chiropodist, or anyone whose specialized services you need? Don't skip the ads of local stores. What prices are being asked for food and clothes and household necessities?

Read the classified ads carefully. They will give you a picture of the kinds of employment available, the prevailing wages, real estate values in different sections of the locality, and local business opportunities should you wish to start your own business, buy into an existing business, or convert a skill or hobby into an income-producer.

If you decide to buy property in the locality, by all means go in person to investigate. Then, however desirable the property may seem to you, do not buy it on your own, but rather through a real estate broker or attorney. An even greater degree of caution should be exercised if you decide to buy into a business. However sound the business may seem to be, no move should be made until you have hired a reputable accounting organization in the area to inspect the firm's books, and have had that organization explain their report to you in detail.

The active, productive middle years are the time to buy such property and build on it, or to invest in such business, so that your retirement home will be ready for you, and your share of the business producing for you by the time you need them.

A retirement home itself can easily be an income-producer. It can be used during these years as a vacation home, or it can be rented and the income banked against the time when we ourselves occupy it.

Two sisters I visited in Wisconsin recently proved themselves foresighted indeed when, many years ago, they came into a small inheritance and used it to build an apartment house. They were young business women then, of excellent character and outstanding employment records, so they had no trouble persuading the bank to add generous backing to their own funds to make the project possible. They chose their site carefully, and built the kind of apartments they had always dreamed of having for themselves. They have seldom had a vacancy through the years. The two sisters occupy a spacious top-floor apartment which looks out over the city. Their investment has given them a good income, security and a rent-free home all during these active years.

One sister retired last spring and the other plans to retire in another year or two. They do not think of it as "retiring" but as being free to devote full time to all the religious and community interests that have occupied their spare time for so long. It cannot help being a happy retirement, with the knowledge that they will never be burdens to anyone, and will be able to devote themselves to the interests and welfare of others.

An apartment house, of course, is an ambitious undertaking and not possible to most of us. We can, however, carry out the idea on a smaller scale in planning our retirement home. A married couple I know built their retirement home as a four-family affair. They are receiving the income now from all four apartments, and when they are ready to move into one of them they will still enjoy the income from three.

Many people are buying or building income-producing retirement homes in resort communities, in sections of the country frequented by summer vacationers or winter sports fans, or near heavy-traffic highways.

Some of these are planned like small inns, designed to accommodate guests during the season. I have seen many of them, both the retirement and the active working variety, up in New Hampshire's White Mountains. The region is a paradise for summer vacationers. It is also the center of winter sports in the East, and all winter long the high slopes are blackened by thousands of skiers who pour out of the frequent ski trains from Boston and New York.

The area is studded with large hotels, smaller inns, tourist homes, cabin colonies, motels and ski barracks, so that there are accommodations to fit every taste and every purse. In fact there is scarcely a private home which does not have at least an extra bedroom or two which can be rented to vacationers. Some of these homes, and many of the cabin colonies and motels, are owned and operated by older people who have retired from active business in other parts of the country, and who are now earning a good income in a place which for years was to them simply a delightful vacation spot.

Several people I know have built retirement homes near small but popular inns. Such inns specialize in delicious food and their large clientele grows larger season by season as the word spreads. They can feed any number, but do not have enough rooms to "sleep" them all. Rather than refer them to other inns or hotels, they are grateful for private homes nearby where their guests can sleep, then return to the inn for meals and activities. The people who accommodate the overflow from these inns find the work both easy and profitable. They need provide no meals for the guests, but only clean rooms and fresh linens.

It must be pointed out, however, that there are risks even in such a community. As in all resort communities, tourists are the principal trade. Residents of New Hampshire's White Mountain region are fortunate in having a double season, with only a few weeks during the spring and fall to repair and replenish before the rush of summer and winter guests. But the winter season depends, as it must, upon the weather. Everyone's concern then is whether there will be enough snow to attract skiers, and whether the snow will come early enough to make a good season possible. Since tourists are the principal trade both summer and winter, business and employment opportunities are confined largely to those services that attract tourists: providing lodging for them or working in one of the existing hotels, opening a shop or finding employment in one of the established shops.

The majority of resort communities have only a single season. This might prove an advantage to many people of retirement age who find that a summer's or a winter's income is sufficient to carry them through the rest of the year. There are many, too, who operate small tourist types of businesses, such as gift shops, who move with the seasons. They conduct their business in a popular summer vacation spot, and then move it south to a winter resort.

Motels have become vastly popular since we in this country have become a mobile population. Back in 1909 when Henry Ford's first Model T—dubbed "Tin Lizzie" with both derision and affection—started chugging up and down the roads of America, none of those who shouted *"Get a horse!"* dreamed that the little black car, ugly and noisy and unpredictable as she was, would play a major part in making America what it is today: a nation of fine highways that have eliminated distance, speeded communication, brought city and country within a tankful of gas from each other, and made us a population-on-wheels in which no man's family need be isolated unless he wishes it. The families of America travel the highways today and are on the lookout for attractive motels along the way where they can get a good meal and comfortable clean accommodations for the night.

Cabins, too, are immensely popular. It is not necessary to build a number of them at once; they can be put up one by one over the years as the earlier ones prove the demand and provide the profit. I know a retired couple who started with one guest cabin a few years ago and who now have six. They bought a modest house for themselves not far from a highway. They did not need to supplement their income, but they had saved money on the house and the large piece of property that came with it, so they built a comfortable cabin in a secluded spot at some distance from the house, and put up a sign announcing that it was available. Results encouraged them to build a second cabin the following year, and then to keep on building.

Another couple, parents of a friend of mine, have lived all their lives in Los Angeles. They built a snug retirement home last year out in the warm dry air of the desert not far from a popular resort town. Their building plans included four modern cabins and all four were occupied during their first season.

Many people who wish to supplement their retirement income by taking in overnight guests live near shrines or historic places that attract many visitors, but where there are often few facilities for housing or feeding those visitors. Others who cannot spare a room provide meals and find that there is always a ready market for good home-cooked food.

Just as retirement homes, their kind and location, should be carefully planned now, so we should be particularly careful if we are going to rely on them for our total or partial income. We should spend much time investigating the possibilities in the area of our choice, talking the matter over with responsible local people, and learning from the experience of others in the area what demand there is for the kind of service we propose to give, what hazards there are, and what income we might reasonably hope to realize. And we should consider whether or not we are the kind of people to give such service successfully.

The basic "musts" for any of us who consider some day inviting guests in on a paying basis are that we enjoy people, have a warm and happy personality, make friends easily and have a genuine desire to serve them. We must be immaculate housekeepers and good handymen if we rent out rooms or cabins or operate a motel. We must be above-average cooks if we are to attract people to the meals we serve, and keep them and their friends coming back to us when they are in our area. More than a few places have gone out of business when they depended upon hired cooks. In the first place, really good cooks demand salaries high enough to wipe out the profits. And they are hard to replace. When they leave, our chief asset disappears.

But being an excellent cook is not enough. We must know how to plan meals as well as how to prepare and serve them, and we must know how and where to buy our supplies. We must be willing to work and have a head for business—because occupied rooms and happy diners can be deceptive. Unless we know how to keep proper accounts and handle income and outlay intelligently, figuring our profits and being alert to tax requirements, we can lose money despite our apparent popularity.

I seem to have stressed, to some degree, the kind of retirement home that will bring us an income in our later years, although there will be many of us who will have no need for an income from such a source. I have done this for two reasons. The first is that so many people who have attained their later years are making their retirement homes support them, totally or partially, and are doing so with enjoyment. They find the work easy since they can pace it to their own energy and decide for themselves how much time they will devote to it each season or each year. They need no special training or education to be thus self-employed. And they can determine, within the limits of location and circumstances, how much or how little income they wish to receive. Many older people, in providing accommodations for guests, find that they do not need to be busy all the time in order to realize enough income to provide for their own modest needs.

The second reason for exploring the possibilities of opening our retirement homes to paying guests, or building cabins or motels for them, is just as practical but even more pertinent. We must never lose sight of the fact that the later years are given us in order that we serve others. There is no more basic service, except for ministering to the sick and poor, than providing food and shelter and friendship to those who are away from home.

Sheltering the homeless is one of the corporal works of mercy. Sheltering the temporarily homeless may not, strictly speaking, come under this definition, but it can well be the occasion for some of the spiritual works of mercy. Time and again, people who have opened their homes and their hearts to paying guests have found opportunities to comfort the sorrowful, to counsel the doubtful, to instruct the ignorant and to admonish the sinner. And they find equal opportunity, in such a retirement home, to practice the other spiritual works: to bear wrongs patiently, to forgive all injuries and to pray for the living and the dead.

If you remember your catechism, you will recall that we are all obliged to perform the works of mercy according to our own ability and the need of our neighbors. And you will remember the big black type that we learned by heart: *All the ordinary deeds done every day to relieve the corporal or spiritual needs of others are true works of mercy, if done in the name of Christ.*

Receiving payment for what we do does not mean that we are working for ourselves instead of for Christ. All our lives we are, or should be, working for Christ. He gave us the opportunity and the obligation to work, as He gave us the head and the heart and the talents to use in His Name for the benefit of our family, our neighbors, our parish and all of society.

Our work is truly satisfying and truly successful (though we often may not see its success except in perspective) only when we do it to the best of our ability, knowing with Whom and for Whom we work. And only when we know that do we realize that the fruits of our labors, the salary or income we receive, is His as well. He means us to use as much of it as is necessary for our own needs, and with the rest to help supply the needs of His other children.

VII

The Greater Good

A FEW MONTHS AGO a governmental agency concerned with housing asked the housewives of the country to write letters telling how they thought houses should be built. The writers of the best letters were invited to Washington to sit down with housing experts and exchange ideas. It seemed to me an excellent idea, because housewives are the only real experts when it comes to gearing a house for family living, comfort and convenience.

I suspect that some similar and sensible approach has been used in building the communities for older people that have been mushrooming in many parts of the country, for most of them have been excellently planned, as if a questionnaire had gone out asking suggestions from elderly persons themselves.

The houses in these communities are compactly built so that they are easy to clean and care for, and they are furnished with the latest labor-saving conveniences. They are built on one floor so that there are no stairs to be climbed. Where there are stairs handgrips are usually provided, just as there are handgrips in the bathroom to prevent dangerous falls. Cabinets and shelves are low and within easy reach, so that no clambering up on a chair or kitchen stool is necessary. In some houses, doorways are wide enough to permit easy passage of a wheelchair, and a ramp takes the place of outside steps. Often a flashing light alerts a person who may be hard of hearing to the ringing of doorbell or telephone. Floors are the safe non-slip variety, and reassuring to those who are no longer as steady on their feet as they once were.

Communities planned for older people are often built around a recreation center that provides opportunities for social get-togethers and activities. Shopping and other conveniences are usually close at hand.

The Chamber of Commerce of any area where such a community exists, or is being planned or built, is eager to answer inquiries. In our own planning for independence, it would be wise to send for information about such communities now, in the locations that interest us, so that we can evaluate this kind of living and determine whether or not we would fit into it.

There is something to be said on both sides of the matter. Certainly, life in communities of this type offers us comforts and conveniences geared to our later years when a slower pace and physical limitations may make them welcome. On the other hand we may find a certain monotony in living in a community of our contemporaries, and miss the stimulation and fresh ideas of younger people.

I know a woman of seventy, recently widowed, who was persuaded by friends to settle in St. Petersburg, Florida. Her friends had decided to spend their retirement years there but she lasted just one month.

"I couldn't stand it any longer," she said. "All the streets are lined with green benches, and all the benches are filled with old people just *sitting*. That's all, just sitting, waiting to die. Give me the bustle of New York any time!"

Yet St. Petersburg and other Florida cities are meccas for thousands upon thousands of those who have retired. As our increasing "over-sixty-five" population spirals upward,

Florida and Southern California and other southern resort areas should enjoy the biggest boom in their history. Old people like their easy pace, their balmy temperatures and bright sun. They find they can live there economically without, for example, having to buy heavy coats and warm clothing that are always a major winter expense farther north. In buying or building homes in these areas they save the expense of central heating and insulation, and in some instances are able to make substantial savings in construction costs.

You may enjoy life in this kind of popular after-retirement spot or among your future contemporaries in a community specifically geared for the later years. But those who do not relish it have, I think, a deeper reason than they are aware of. They admit to feeling a kind of frustration at living among their contemporaries, that they attribute to the slowed-down pace and the lack of stimulation that continuing contacts with younger people provide. Actually, their feelings of frustration may stem from the limits this kind of living seems to place upon their opportunities to be needed, which is one of the basic needs of our later years.

Since we are meant to spend our later years in service to others, according to our abilities and their needs, we can of course do this wherever we find ourselves. In a housing community or a town of old people there are many opportunities, but in such places where so much is done for the aged, these opportunities are not always evident. They must be looked for, because loneliness and fear and spiritual needs lie deep. Only those who are aware of the significance of service to others in their own later years will go looking. The rest will accept the comforts and conveniences they find, but never be quite content. They will feel a lack of purpose and thus of meaning in their lives. Without the service to others that proves they are needed and wanted, social activities gradually lose their appeal. The end is "just sitting," as my friend expressed it. And when one "just sits," whether on a bench outdoors or a chair in one's own living room, loneliness and selfishness sit close on either side.

If it is possible for us to be independent in our later years and to choose where we shall live, we may find our physical limitations such that we need the special conveniences offered by houses planned for older people. We may need wheelchair-wide doorways with ramps leading to them, the security of non-slip floors and handgrips and a flashing light to summon us to the telephone. If we find that we cannot safely live alone without such conveniences, and if we can afford them, we can be sure that God has given us these needs because we are needed where they can be supplied. All through life God has a way of bringing together, through physical needs, those who are in spiritual need and those who can help supply such need.

We are, in truth, kindergartners in the spiritual life. Before a child can read, he is given picture books to fit his understanding. That is why we are given picture books to help us understand our faith—our crucifixes, the Stations of the Cross that line the walls of our parish church, our statues and stained-glass windows, the religious pictures in our home, even the little medals we wear. And we are given pictures to help us understand our neighbors. We can see a lame leg or a deafened ear, but we cannot see a lame and lonely soul, nor a spirit that has become deafened to the promptings of grace. It is by ministering to those in physical need that we come to understand their spiritual need and open, through acts of generosity and kindness, channels through which help can flow.

I was once dreadfully afraid of trying to help anyone I

knew to be in spiritual need. It was not so much a fear of being rebuffed as a fear of being inept. I was afraid of talking about spiritual things partly because I could not do it without sounding "preachy" and I knew that preaching would turn from me the person I was trying to help. Mostly I was afraid of being questioned, because I knew that I was neither a theologian nor a philosopher. What if I gave the wrong answers? I might do more harm than good. What if I could not answer at all? The other person might not realize that my own ignorance was responsible, but feel that God, or my Catholic faith, had no answer for his problem.

"Better say nothing," I thought, "than to say the wrong thing, or to have no answer."

What I did not realize was that God knows, even better than we know, that we ordinary laymen are neither theologians nor philosophers. Yet He has given each of us the job of bringing others to Him. I knew He could not make our eternal salvation dependent upon an impossible job, and that He always supplies full and sufficient means for carrying out His commands. It took a long time for me to understand that God does indeed bid us to bring others to Him, but to do it with the means at hand—not as theologians or philosophers but simply as the people we are.

He has given the least of us the seeds of His truth, and seeds are meant to be sown. Only if they are sown can they grow into souls. The thought frightens me sometimes. I picture myself arriving at the gate of Heaven, still clutching my little bag of seeds, and being turned back.

"Sorry," I can hear St. Peter saying, "you can't come in here with seeds. Why didn't you plant them? You should have known that, as seeds, they would bar your way to Heaven. Only as souls will they let you in."

I picture, too, the little door that leads into Heaven. I have a feeling that however much we may be trimmed down to fit it, it will still be difficult for us to get through alone. If we arrive there by ourselves, there will be a good deal of explaining to do, and explanations have a way of falling flat at such a time. But if we arrive in the goodly company of souls we have helped in one way or another, the door will swing wide and we shall find our reception joyful beyond all imagining.

How, then, are we to reach and help these souls in need? They cannot be reached by theology or philosophy, even if we had it to give them, and had eloquence besides. They can be reached simply and solely by love.

If we use God's formula, and act *as if* we love them, we shall come to love them sooner than we think. And, perhaps to our surprise, we shall find our love returned. We may not be able to preach, but preaching has never been so effective as good example, and there is not one of us, however inarticulate or unlettered, who cannot preach the most eloquent sermon in the shining terms of a good life. Further, there is not one of us who cannot reach deep into the troubled soul of another with the healing and hopeful touch of love. Our speech may stumble and our fingers fumble, but love is steady and sure and unfailing.

Old people, like children, are most in need of love. It follows, therefore, that there will be more opportunities for loving service where there is a concentration of old people.

There is a simple rule to remember: where we settle down is not as important as why we settle down where we do. We must be guided by the needs of others. This does not mean that we must play the martyr and overlook our own needs. Our own needs are good because God gave them to us, and one of the reasons He gave them to us is to lead us through them to the place where we can best minister to others, and also to give us through them the understanding we must have to reach these others.

But it is important, too, to remember that souls cannot be measured by a mathematical yardstick. Two souls are not worth twice as much as one soul because each individual soul is of infinite worth. Therefore the many souls who may need us in a community of older people are not necessarily worth, in God's eyes, more than the single soul who may need us at home, down the street or around the corner, in our neighborhood or our parish. We must base our plans for independent living in our later years upon the needs of others, realizing that from this distance there would seem to be many more needs where many old people are gathered together, but remembering that our plans may be subject to change, when the time comes, because of the need of a single neighbor. There will be no confusion, no difficulty in evaluating, no trying to balance the one need against the many needs to determine our course. God will show us, through our own needs and circumstances, what we must do.

It is a delicate weighing process, this balancing of good against good, and we are not equipped to do it because we cannot use God's yardstick to measure which is the greater good.

The problem of the "greater good" used to trouble me a lot. There are so many choices in a parish. Is it better, I used to wonder, to spend an hour in the parish hall with the women making bandages that would comfort a number of unknown cancer victims, or to spend that hour bringing the comfort of companionship to just one cancer victim down the street? Is it better to spend a day collecting clothes for the war-ravaged children of Europe or Korea, or to spend that day dressing and feeding and caring for the children in the house around the corner where the mother is bedridden? Should the very real needs of the poor and sick and spiritually starved natives of far-off lands come before the very real needs of the poor and sick and spiritually starved natives of our own parish?

Actually, there's no "either-or" choice. It's a simple matter of putting first things first, of remembering where charity begins and that unless charity sinks firm roots at home and in the home parish, its growth is apt to be spindly and hollow outside. Just as a mother cannot in conscience spend her days sewing for poor children while her own children run ragged, we cannot embark upon great and far-flung projects while little projects close to home cry for attention —and are too often overlooked because they are not projects but only people and they cry silently.

It may seem strange to speak of the work we do in our later years, when we may be severely limited in one or many ways, as a great and far-flung project. The work we do may seem utterly insignificant to us, but God has a different way of measuring. We measure by the amount of effort we expend, and by the visible results of our efforts. He measures by the amount of love we put into any effort, and often saves the results to surprise us with when we reach His little door.

Some of us may indeed be able to start needed "projects" in a community of older people where such projects may help many of them: launching community activities or socials, sharing our skills with others by teaching something we know to those who would like to learn, such as a handicraft, a language, a love of books or music. More likely our help will lie simply in providing companionship and conversation through which our interest and love can flow. If we are denied even the activity of visiting others, the greatest help of all can be the example we give of a life informed by faith, shorn of complaints and self-interest, turned upward in gratitude to God and outward to express that gratitude in love of those around us. Because being is more important than doing, what we are is more important than where we are.

I often think of us Catholics as sparks in a dry wood. God has set us here in order to enkindle the earth. That does not mean that He expects any one of us to set the world on fire, but He does expect each of us at least to enkindle the splinters around us. If we do that much, He will do the rest. It is not a job confined to our active middle years. It is a job we are expected to do, and to do well, as long as we live. There is a compulsory retirement age, but it differs with each of us—because the day of our retirement is the day of our death. And if we have done our job well, we will not be given the customary gold watch (for there is no time to measure in Heaven) but something a great deal more valuable.

The service we give to others in our later years need not be limited, of course, to other old people, just as the service we give to others now is not limited to them. We need only look around us to see old people giving joyous service to the young.

A neighbor of mine is a grandmother several times over. She taught school until she reached retirement age four or five years ago, and retired just in time to see her husband through his final illness. Widowed, and with her children and grandchildren settled in their own homes, she felt a tremendous emptiness. It was not the negative kind of emptiness that is mere absence of activity, but a positive and gnawing kind of emptiness that needed to be filled. She could have lived comfortably for the rest of her days on her pension, the insurance her husband had left and other benefits. But she knew that she had many more valuable years to give to the children she loved.

Too old to return to teaching in the public school system,

she applied to a school operated by the state for problem and delinquent children, set in the midst of square miles of farmland and woods. The authorities were impressed, when they interviewed her, not only by her qualifications as a teacher but by her evident love for children. She proved her love when she found that there was no opening at the time for a teacher by accepting a job as housemother for one of the cottages of delinquent teen-age girls. She has never been happier in her life. Nor have the girls.

Many people, even young and active teachers, haven't the courage to take on such a difficult job. These girls are of many shades of delinquency, but arrive at the school with a uniform defiance of authority. The inner scars of their experiences, constantly being picked at and irritated by their fear and insecurity, show up in sullen behavior, frequent fights and constant plots to "escape." They are uncommunicative and uncooperative. But my neighbor has wrought a great change, in her own cottage at least. She must, and does, maintain discipline, but she knows that discipline without love is worthless. It is because she loves her girls, and they know they are loved, that she is able to maintain discipline and to make of it an open door to a better life for her girls rather than a locked door to confine them.

It may be, in the divine scheme of things, that all her active years of teaching were but a preparation for the most important work of her life, now taking place in that tiny cottage tucked away among the trees. It may be, too, that all the work of our own young and middle years, important as it seems to us, is but a preparation for our real work which still lies ahead.

There is a fireman in our parish who retired some years ago. He and his wife had never had children, but he has been "uncle" to generations of children in the neighborhood. Many of his friends in the fire department had retired to Florida, and he and his wife had always planned to join them there. But when the time came, he knew he was needed here instead. The children needed him: his "Little League" baseball team that he had coached pretty close to the championship, the high schoolers whom he is helping to build a clubhouse, his "Junior Citizenship" activities with groups in the area, his work for the parish confraternity, and the "good talks" that make his house and back yard a popular gathering spot for neighborhood boys. During his busiest years I doubt that he was more active or more happy than he is in his busy "retirement."

A retired businessman I know, now crippled with arthritis, could be spending his days in a warmer climate and enjoying conveniences especially planned for his age and physical limitations. But he has chosen to remain home, because he has found that being needed brings him greater satisfaction than mere enjoyment. He earns a small income by making out tax returns for individuals and for the shop owners in the neighborhood. Freely and gladly given, however, is the advice that keeps his home well supplied with visitors. Young people come to discuss their prospects with him, and to ask his help in preparing résumés to present to prospective employers. Older people come to him with business problems, or just to talk.

A little old lady I once visited has been able to help others by apparently letting them help her. She is totally blind now, and confined to her small apartment. Over the years she has built up a regular schedule of young "readers," each with an appointed hour during the week when he or she reads aloud. The youngsters, though they may have been tempted originally by the refreshments served at the end of each hour of reading, take tremendous pride in their work. They arrive promptly as scheduled and are both considerate and conscientious. Results of their responsibility and of their unselfish service have become evident in other areas. Their parents report that they are more considerate of other people generally, are more willing to help around the house, and are getting better marks in school because of increased attention to their school work.

The old lady is responsible for the improvement. Before adding a young reader to her list (she has an eager waiting list by this time) she checks with the parents. What sort of help does Johnnie or Joanie need most? The reading matter she chooses for each, and listens to with such apparent enjoyment, is selected to give each reader the help he needs. It helps him even more to think that he is helping her. It is a varied diet, and she flourishes on it. She may be "taught" a youngster's catechism one hour, be plunged into American history the next or in some book she has chosen to light the pages of the child's history textbook and bring its great men to life, and perhaps suggest to her next reader some "stuffy classic" on his supplementary school reading list so that she may infect him with her enthusiasm for great literature.

We don't have to look far for people in need of something we can supply. But we should not begin looking for them when the weight of our own years starts to dim our eyesight, or we shall not find them. Spiritual insight, too, has a way of dimming when it is not given constant exercise. If all our years are spent in outgoing service to others we shall be guided, through our own needs and circumstances, to the specific service God has appointed for our later years. It will be a service that illumines those later years and gives them joyous meaning, because it will be both our flowering and our fulfilment.

VIII

"*On Our Way Rejoicing*"

Do you remember the Tower of Babel, where everyone started to talk different languages until the project fell apart in confusion? I think our modern world is something like that; although we may speak the same language, none of us means exactly the same thing by the same words.

It is, in a way, impossible that we should mean exactly the same thing, for a word or a concept must enter into our minds in order that we be aware of it. And when it has done that it becomes personalized. We shape it according to our knowledge and experiences and wrap it around with our emotions, so that what comes out of us differs—though it sounds the same—from what comes out of others, just as they all differ from the original kernel of truth that lies under so many expressions.

One of these expressions is "old folks' home." I cannot say it or hear it without feeling depressed and smelling disinfectant. Certainly no one who knows today's homes for old people should have such feelings. If you have a similar distaste, knowing that there is no reason for it, you can probably trace it back to a far-off incident as I did.

It happened when I was a little girl singing in the choir of the Protestant church I then attended. Twice a year, on Christmas and at Easter, our choir would go out to sing at

the "old folks' home." Scrubbed and shining in our starched
white dresses, we would take a bus and fill it with happy
chatter during the ride to the outskirts of the city. But
the chatter would die away as the big, gray, stone building
came in sight. A kind of gloom would settle upon us. We
would walk silently up to the big door and open it to a
smell that was partly soap, partly cooking (invariably vegetable soup—and I haven't eaten vegetable soup to this day),
but mostly disinfectant.

There was an odd yellow light about the place because the
upper parts of all the windows were made of yellow glass.
Perhaps the effect had been intended to be that of cheery
sunlight, but to me it was the yellow light that often
precedes a storm; it was foreboding, and full of decay and
death. The floors were bare and scrubbed and we clattered
over them to the big recreation room. I thought I had
never known a room so misnamed. It too was bare and cold
as a barn and furnished with nothing but an ancient
upright piano and a number of hard benches. The oldest
people I had ever seen filled the hard benches, looking so
pleased to see us that I was dreadfully embarrassed.

At Christmas time we sang carols and at Easter we sang
hymns, and I was further embarrassed when the old people
kept time with their hands and feet and crutches, and
especially when their quavering voices joined in the familiar
songs.

We were pleased, in a way, to be there, and proud to be
the center of attention. But we could not wait to get out.
We had a traditional way of leaving the place. We would go
single file down the line of old people, wishing them a Merry
Christmas or a Happy Easter as the case might be, and then
line up at the door. The choirmaster would hum a note
to give us the pitch; then we would march out singing a
hymn. It was always the same hymn. I have forgotten all

of it except for the first line: *"On our way rejoicing, as we homeward move. . . ."*

No words were more suited to our feelings at that moment. We did indeed rejoice that we were on our way home. Our young voices were stronger and surer and happier than they had been during the whole preceding hour. We were on our way away from decay and disinfectant and that eerie yellow gloom. We had had a job to do, and now we had the good feeling that we had done it and it was over with. The world outside was bright with Christmas snow or Easter budding, alive with the excitement of all our young interests, and we rejoiced.

The strange thing is that so many of us act the same way today. The old folks' homes that abound on every side bear not the slightest resemblance to the one I used to visit. They are filled with bright chintz, comfortable chairs, color and movement and cheer, and old people busy with activities. Many of us put our old people into these homes where we visit them on occasion. We do not relish the visiting hour we spend with them, but we have the job to do and we feel good when we do it. We feel especially good when we see the care they are getting and the facilities of the home. When we stop at the desk on the way out to pay the stiff bill that is waiting for us, we feel that we are doing all that any children could be asked to do for their parents. Satisfied and a bit smug, we go on our way rejoicing.

Not all of us do so, of course, and not all old folks' homes allow old people to be "put there" by others. But enough do to make what are today called "nursing homes" among the most profitable commercial enterprises in the country.

It comes back once again to the Golden Rule and the Fourth Commandment. What we do unto our mothers and fathers now is apt to be done unto us when our time comes.

We are commanded to honor them; to give them love, respect and care. They must be in that order. If we love, then respect and care will follow because they flow naturally from our love. Respect and care without love, a situation so common today that we are in danger of accepting it as a norm, is the cold providing of necessities from our pockets rather than our hearts. Without love to warm the giving our gifts can be resented and our old people made to feel unwanted. Care alone, without either love or respect, is tragic, and tragically common. Its results have filled the commercial nursing homes that have proved so profitable that they are mushrooming on every side.

In all fairness it must be noted that there are many good commercial nursing homes that abide by existing legislation and give conscientious care. Some go beyond the minimum requirements. It cannot be held against them that they make a profit, for they are business ventures that are well run in order to make a legitimate profit. But we must note, too, that there are many such homes that hide a multitude of evils under a pleasant exterior, and that manage to make an even more handsome profit.

Not long ago, I attended a dinner at which there were a number of top businessmen. The man sitting next to me was a manufacturer, founder and head of his firm, who was about to retire although he was only in his early fifties.

"I own three nursing homes for old people," he told me. "I can retire comfortably on those three alone. Actually, the reason I am retiring is to build more. The three I have are full and each has a waiting list. I am building wings on two of them which will about double their capacity, and I'm leaving for Florida at the end of the month to supervise one under construction—a new conception in nursing homes, as luxurious as a fine hotel. Four more are in the blueprint stage."

My curiosity was aroused and I questioned him. I was particularly curious because not long before scandalous conditions in some nursing homes had made headlines in the newspapers and an investigation was underway.

Among conditions revealed were excessive charges: items such as fifty cents each for aspirin tablets, and the like. Some homes had far fewer registered nurses per number of patients than the law required; one chain of several homes under the same ownership was discovered to have "prop" nurses. They were registered nurses, the reports stated, who operated on a free-lance basis between the homes. Actually on the staff of none of them, the nurses were on call whenever it was learned that the inspectors were due. They would arrive at the home shortly before the inspectors, bustle around efficiently, then be shipped off to the next home, sometimes beating the inspectors there by minutes. I had wondered, while reading the accounts, how the inspectors had failed to recognize the nurses. I speculated that perhaps the inspectors were particularly non-observant, or particularly well paid—though not on the books—or that the free-lance pool of cooperating nurses was sufficiently large to permit different groups of nurses to appear at each home for the few minutes required for the inspection.

I mentioned these reports to the manufacturer I met at dinner.

"Yes, of course," he said. "We've been following these accounts and unfortunately there is some truth in them. We need much stiffer controls. Those of us who try to run legitimate places resent these shady practices most of all because they hurt our business. Providing for the aged today is one of the most profitable fields anyone can get into. It's a booming market, with no end in sight, and the money to be made attracts all kinds of people. Anybody can build a nursing home today and have a reasonable hope of seeing it

filled the first week, if not the first day. There's no limit to
the demand—though, I must say, the demand isn't on the
part of the old people."

"What do you mean?" I asked. "Aren't old people the
whole reason behind the boom?"

"Naturally, the demand itself is being created by the
increasing numbers of old people," he said. "What I mean
is that the old people themselves don't ask to be put into
these nursing homes. Their children put them in. Either
there's no room for them at home, or if there is room the
old people put a damper on the children's activities—
entertaining, vacationing, traveling, that type of thing.
That's what makes it so discouraging at times.

"In my own nursing homes, for example, our charges
are not excessive, we observe every legal requirement,
and we do everything we can to give the old people the
best of care and keep them comfortable and content. Yet
you should hear them on visiting days. When the children
come the old folks weep and wail and beg to be taken
home as if they were in prison and we were maltreating
them."

"It must be discouraging," I agreed, "but what can you
do about it?"

"Frankly, I don't know," he said. "I do know that it's not
our fault. And it's not the old people's fault, either. I blame
the children. By paying out the weekly fee, and, in those
homes that require it, a substantial entrance fee, the children feel that they are doing everything possible for their
parents. Their consciences are at rest because they are sure
that they are proving themselves to be 'good children' by
paying for parents' care. Many of them even cut down on
their visits and show up less and less frequently, because the
old people make them feel that what they are doing is not
appreciated."

"And you blame the children?" I asked.

"I do indeed," he replied. "I'm not the one to say this, because it would kill my business, but I rate children who put unwilling parents into a home so that they can wash their hands of their care as little better than criminals. I know the kind of care the old people get in the homes I own. I know it is good care and that there is nothing in our treatment or facilities to make them unhappy. They are unhappy because they know very well that they are not wanted by their own children. They want love; they want to be home no matter how crowded their presence might make it. It's lack of love, not lack of care, that kills them."

It was, I thought, an observant statement, coming as it did from a man who admitted that he was guided by no religious or humanitarian principles, but by shrewd business judgment alone.

Planning and providing for old people in terms of physical care are not enough. It takes love to give us the wisdom to plan with them, not for them. Entering a home for the aged should be their own decision, just as we shall want to be free to choose such a life for ourselves some day. It may indeed be our choice, because we may find that a properly chosen home offers advantages more particularly suited to our needs than do housing communities for the aged, or resort communities that attract old people.

But a home for the aged should be carefully chosen. This involves two things. First, we should take a little time out of our present active years to visit a number of these homes and bring ourselves up-to-date on them. They will be eye-openers in many cases, and we will find them dissolving the distaste and correcting the twisted impressions in which we have kept our concept of "old folks' home" wrapped for so long. Then we should make careful note of the details about each of the homes we visit: our impressions of the place, the attitude of residents with whom we talk, the requirements for entrance and the cost of living there, the qualifications of the management and staff, the facilities offered, the regulations under which the place is operated and the rules under which the residents live.

I have visited homes for the aged that are so truly all that a home should be, and where I have seen such happiness on the part of the residents, that I have sometimes wished—especially when my work has piled high and I am under frantic pressure to get out from under it—that I could just pack my bags and move in on the spot. This despite the fact that my childhood impressions are so deeply imbedded that I still feel the depression when I hear the words "old folks' home." But I know my feelings bear no relation to present reality, and so I am able to relegate them to a pigeonhole which is concerned only with matters long past.

Despite childhood impressions (mine, at any rate), life in a modern well-run home for the aged can be pleasant indeed. Rather than being "nursing homes," the good ones are more like actual homes with nursing facilities on the premises. Thus the old people who are perfectly well may live there happily, and those who are not well or who become bedridden may have the care and treatment they require more conveniently and more continuously than would be possible if each lived in his own home.

Opportunities for service to others are perhaps greater in a home for the aged than in other communities of old people. Even though so much is done for them that their needs, as in the other types of communities, are not always evident, they are bound to become evident to us because we live so closely with them. We cannot fail to become aware of them, if we ourselves have cultivated a spirit of awareness, through the weeks and months of constant association and observation. Launching or participating in community activities, as well as visiting back and forth, and the ability to perform acts of kindness and helpfulness, are much easier because we are all under one roof. We need but step across the hall to visit a neighbor in need, just as we have but to go down the corridor to join other neighbors undergoing treatment or therapy, or go downstairs to meet them in chapel, at meals, and share community recreation and activities with them.

If it is important to investigate the various types of living available for our later years now, so that we can make a wise choice when the time comes, it is even more important to investigate homes for the aged during our middle years. If we should choose this type of living we must make our choice before the time comes. The better homes have long waiting lists. Because they are good homes, the old people who live there seldom leave. And also because they are good their old people are long-lived, so openings must be bespoken well in advance.

I cannot guess God's plans for me in my later years, nor do I want to try. If it should be a home for the aged, He may well put me into one of the commercial homes where abuses run rampant, and my work will be clear-cut: attempting to correct the abuses, or comforting those who suffer under them, or perhaps doing no more than giving good example by accepting what I cannot change with patience and good cheer.

But if the choice of such a home were up to me I should look for one kind only: a home run and staffed by nuns. I would not need to look for happy attitudes or attributes, for proper qualifications or facilities. I would know by the presence of the nuns that these things are present. And I would know something far more important: where nuns are, love is.

It is not because I am a Catholic that I should want to be cared for by nuns in my later years. It is because nuns work for love. They are totally dedicated to those in their care, because they are totally dedicated to Christ Whom they see in every patient, the young and the old, the sick and the well and the poor.

I like the often-told but nonetheless true story of the man who saw a nun cleaning and dressing the injuries of a body so terribly mangled that the man himself became sick at the sight.

"Sister," he said, "I wouldn't do that for a million dollars."

Sister looked at him quietly.

"Neither would I," she said.

Non-Catholics, too, know and love our nuns, and seek their care. They flood our Catholic hospitals and homes for the aged, knowing that they are welcome regardless of creed. Though Catholics make up, roughly, only one-fifth of the American community, Catholic hospitals make up twenty-seven per cent of all voluntary non-profit hospitals in this country, and care for a third of all the patients in these hospitals, this third amounting last year alone to almost eight and a half million people.

I have seen Protestant and Jewish parents, as well as non-believers, bring their children to the nuns when they needed specialized care, such as schools for the deaf or the blind or the mentally retarded, knowing that along with expert care, their children would be given total devotion and be surrounded by love.

An example of the awakening of one non-Catholic who had never before had any contact with nuns is given in a recently published book that tells a mother's simple and moving story about her crippled daughter Nancy.[1] Thirteen-

---

[1] Marguerite Hamilton, *Red Shoes for Nancy* (Philadelphia: J. B. Lippincott Co., 1955).

year-old Nancy, who died just recently, was the victim of
a rare congenital blood disease which had been responsible for more than forty operations and the amputation of
both legs and the fingers of one hand. Her brief life had
been spent in and out of hospitals. They were years of heartbreak for her mother, who had grown up without a faith to
sustain her and to give meaning to such hardship. It was
not until Nancy entered a Catholic hospital that her mother
began to glimpse a divine purpose in Nancy's affliction.
There is a moving account in her book of her wonder at the
treatment Nancy received there:

"I couldn't quite grasp the situation," she writes, "but I
sensed that an entirely new way of living was opening up
for us. I looked on in wonder, visit after visit, at the way
everyone treated Nancy, until finally I had to ask about it.
I was still too much in awe of the Sisters to feel entirely
comfortable talking to them. They were the friendliest and
most gracious people I had ever known, but their formal
attire seemed to set them apart from ordinary folk. . . . But
I summoned my courage one day, and followed one of them
down the hall just after she had stopped to speak to Nancy.

" 'Sister,' I said, 'may I speak to you?'

" 'Of course.' She turned and her eyes lighted. 'Why,
you're Nancy's mother!'

" 'Yes,' I said, wondering how to go on. 'I just wanted to
tell you how much I appreciate how nice everybody is being to Nancy. You all seem to go out of your way, as if she
were somebody special—not a charity patient, I mean.'

"I stopped awkwardly, and felt my face flushing with
embarrassment. What had I said? Had I implied that Sister
thought Nancy was a paying guest, and wouldn't have
been so kind if she had known otherwise?

"Sister laughed, and it was like the tinkle of silvery bells
down the marble hallway.

" 'Yes, Mrs. Hamilton,' she said. 'Nancy is a charity patient. I wonder if you know what a charity patient is?'

"It was my turn to laugh, a little bitterly.

" 'Do I know what a charity patient is?' I asked. 'Why, that's all Nancy's ever been. We've never been able to pay. It's always had to be charity. Free, I mean.'

" 'Oh, no,' said Sister, 'charity doesn't mean free.'

"I could feel a sudden fear pinching me around the heart. If charity didn't mean free, Nancy would have to leave, and we'd be in debt the rest of our lives for what she'd already received.

" 'No,' Sister was saying, 'charity doesn't mean free at all. Charity means *love*.'

" '*Love?*' I asked. I must have looked astonished, because Sister gave her gentle little laugh again.

" 'Of course,' she said. 'Don't you remember what St. Paul said—faith, hope, and charity, and the greatest of these is charity? Charity means love. And a charity patient is a patient we care for out of love, not for money. You can't pay for love, you know.' "

No, it is not because I am a Catholic that I hope that the nuns care for me, if I some day need care. I think non-Catholics, particularly those with little or no faith, need their love more than I do, and it may be that God will ask me to surrender my place to one of them.

Nor is it because I hope to be a "charity" patient, in the sense in which Mrs. Hamilton used the term and in which most of us think of it. Patients in Catholic hospitals and homes for the aged pay standard rates, or pay according to their means, and what they pay is needed for operating costs and equipment. But the nuns themselves work for love, and whether a patient pays much or little or nothing at all makes not the slightest difference in the love and care he receives. The wealthiest patient is not wealthy enough to buy such devotion. And the poorest patient is not too poor to have it lavished upon him in piled-up and brimming-over measure.

When I was a child I used to leave the "old folks' home" rejoicing. If I should find myself entering one some day—not just for an hour of singing but for years of living—and if I should see a nun standing at the door in welcome, the words of the old hymn would again lighten my step.

> *"On our way rejoicing,"* my heart would sing, *"as we homeward move. . . ."*

Because I'd know I was truly moving homeward.

And I would rejoice.

—·—

IX

The Little Things

I LIKE TO THINK of the Hancocks as my friends although I visited them only once. Their name is not Hancock but it will do to protect their privacy, for I imagine this gentle old couple might be startled to find themselves in a book.

I dropped in on them about ten o'clock one morning. Mrs. Hancock opened the door, her slim erect figure silhouetted against the blaze of sunlight that streamed into their attractive living-bedroom.

"Come in, come in," she said in welcome. "I'm so glad you came early because it gives us time to talk. We have such a busy day ahead."

A little breeze from the river ruffled the curtains as I went in. The sunlight was reflected from lovingly polished furniture, silver-framed family photographs and crisp flowered chintz that made me feel I was walking into a garden.

"What a *happy* room!" I exclaimed.

Mrs. Hancock smiled. "It's happy," she said, "because we're happy in it."

Mr. Hancock rose from his chair, disturbing the lazy halo of pipe smoke that had been wreathing his head. He clicked off the television news program he had been watching and brought over a chair for me. His wife excused herself, then was back in a few minutes with coffeepot, cups and a generous wedge of coffeecake.

"I'm sure you can have a little second breakfast with us," she said. "We start the day early with Mass at seven and breakfast at quarter of eight. A cup of coffee tastes good just about now."

Over the coffee, I asked them about the busy day they were planning. "What do you do with your time?" I inquired.

"Time?" Mr. Hancock chuckled. "I wish we had more of it."

"My husband has a treatment at eleven o'clock," said Mrs. Hancock, "and I have an appointment at the beauty parlor at the same time. Then this afternoon, after dinner, I have a millinery class—I'm making my own Easter hat, you know. It's going to be a surprise for Henry."

Mr. Hancock looked skeptical. "I don't surprise so easily after forty-nine years of marriage," he said to me. "We're celebrating our golden wedding anniversary a year from June." Then, turning to her: "What kind of hat are you planning for *that?*"

"I think I'll let you design that one, Henry," Mrs. Hancock said. "Your favorite color and everything. You tell me what you like best, and I'll make it."

"Speaking of anniversaries," he said, "we mustn't forget to stop in at the hospital this afternoon. The Healeys would have been celebrating theirs sometime this month."

"Yes, we must see Mary. Her husband died a few months ago," Mrs. Hancock explained to me, "just short of their golden anniversary. Now she's in the hospital with a heart condition. It helps when folks remember. Her mind's probably full of it—the anniversary I mean. Henry, it would be nice to take her some flowers; not flowers for being in the hospital, but fixed up specially, like an anniversary."

"How about a bridal bouquet?"

"Henry, that's a *wonderful* idea! Do you want to go and have it made up, or shall I?"

"You'd better," he said, "because I have a special committee meeting right after dinner to arrange the performance for next week. Then I have to be at the dentist at three, and I have my painting class at four."

"Well, I'll go and get it after millinery class. I have a little while then, before the card party. I did want to get the scrapbook finished before the children come, but that can wait."

"Our oldest son and his wife are bringing the children over after supper," Mr. Hancock said. "We're taking them to an entertainment tonight—Broadway stars, and good music. Refreshments afterward. It should be a nice evening. We do it every little while, and we all enjoy it."

I had long since ceased to speak. I just looked, listened and hoped that my astonishment did not show. The Hancocks must have been in their late seventies but their enthusiasm was that of newlyweds. Their eyes sparkled with anticipation of the day's activities, a busy round that tired me just to think of it.

The little ship's clock on the mantel showed quarter of eleven, and I rose to go.

"Come in again," urged Mrs. Hancock. "We like company."

"I'd love to," I said. "Maybe on a day when you're not so busy."

She laughed. "Every day is just as full as this one. I can't imagine anything worse than an empty day. Why, there wouldn't be anything to get out of bed for!"

I closed the door of their little home and walked down the hall to the elevator. Sister was waiting for me at the desk in the lobby.

"Amazing!" I said, shaking my head. "If I could only hope to be as lively and as interested in everything when I get to be their age!"

"I thought you'd like the Hancocks," Sister said. "But remember, they're not exceptional—at least not here. I could have sent you to visit other married couples, or to dozens of single people, and you would have found them all happy and busy. Come, let me show you around. You'll get some idea of what they do and what's done for them."

I followed Sister in wonder. For just an instant my mind went back to the yellow gloom and the smell of disinfectant that were forever linked, in my memory, to the home for the aged I had visited as a child. How incongruous, I thought, in a place like this! This, too, was a home for the aged, one of a dozen in the New York area affiliated with Catholic Charities. The Hancocks' cheerful home had been on one of the upper floors, and all the activities they were planning would be taking place somewhere in the building.

The heart of the building was the beautiful chapel. I liked the idea of having to go through it to get from one wing to another, giving one a brief brush with Reality frequently during the day, and serving as a reminder to people going through it of why they were going where they were, and the meaning that gave purpose and direction and light to all their busy goings and comings.

We went through the big attractive dining rooms.

"One of the most important things," said Sister, "is to get our guests to *eat*. Many of them eat well, finding food a constant pleasure that doesn't dim with advancing years as so many other pleasures do. It's a great comfort to them and that's good. But many others have to be coaxed and catered to because the proper food is important to them. We've had old folks come here who for years have not eaten properly. I remember one woman who was the despair of her family. She refused to eat meals with the family, although her daughter planned and cooked them well and tried to include many of her mother's favorite dishes. Instead, she'd pick at things in the kitchen all day long—a bite of this and a nibble of that, whatever appealed to her. Many old folks do that, and such a deficient diet is dangerous. When she came to us she was seriously undernourished and had to be retrained in good eating habits. It took some time but we finally succeeded. You should see her now—she's first at the table!"

Through the glass door of an office I glimpsed a Sister in a white habit.

"She's our dietitian," said Sister. "Come, let me show you the week's menus. We have them posted in the kitchen. They may surprise you."

They did indeed surprise me. They were as tempting and varied as the menus of a fine hotel. "Calves' liver with bacon curls," I read. "Chicken potpie with flaky crust, filet of sole with sauce amandine, veal cutlets."

I looked around the spotless kitchen, and saw what seemed to be another kitchen beyond.

"Yes," said Sister, "we have several kitchens. One is a complete bakeshop; we bake our own bread, rolls and pastries."

We walked through, watching men in white uniforms with tall chefs' caps busying themselves over shining counter expanses of stainless steel, working at the stoves and the great ovens, pulling crisp-crusted loaves of bread from the bake ovens and lining them up on rolling racks to cool.

At the end of a corridor on the main floor was a huge auditorium with a stage, theater seats and a giant television set.

"This is a busy place, afternoons and evenings," Sister explained. "We show the latest movies here and Broadway stars often come to put on performances for us. We have lots of professional entertainment. And of course we put on our own performances too—you'd be surprised how much talent there is among our guests. Afternoons, there's always an exciting bingo game going on in here. And, though many of our guests have television sets in their rooms, they like coming to watch programs together on our giant screen, especially when the fights are on."

Near the auditorium were two smartly decorated lounges filled with small tables and chairs.

"These are our 'night clubs,'" Sister laughed. "They're filled every evening with our guests and *their* guests. Down the hall we have a regular soda parlor with a soda fountain, a snack bar, even a juke box. We keep two fountain men busy day and evening. It's a popular place for ice cream and sodas, or a cup of tea with a sandwich or a hamburg. How they love snacks!"

On the way back along the corridor we passed a room where a number of old men and women were talking around a long table.

"That's part of our committee," said Sister. "Our guests really run things here. They elect the members of the committee and submit all requests and suggestions to them. The committee weighs the various suggestions, considers the justification of complaints if there are any, and presents those they feel merit attention to the Board. To date, they have all been acted upon. The guests put out their own newspaper too, you know."

I heard a piano being played nearby with such evident musicianship that I thought it must be coming over a radio. Sister smiled and opened the door of a huge room. An old woman sat at a grand piano, almost dwarfed by it, so absorbed in her playing that she didn't see us.

"How beautifully she plays!" I exclaimed.

"Yes," said Sister, "she's one of our guests. She was a concert pianist, and often gives recitals for us. Many of our musician-guests practice in here, and others who are beginners take lessons here—we keep all the musical instruments down at the end there. We have an orchestra and a band too. Actually, this is our ballroom. The old folks love to dance. When it comes to square dancing the room can hardly hold them, big as it is."

I stopped in surprise as we came to a smart little millinery shop.

"What a wonderful idea!" I said. "The women don't have to go out of the building to buy their hats."

"Buy them, have them made, make them themselves, remodel them, freshen them up—just about everything," said Sister. "The ladies love their hats. We have a milliner here every afternoon. She made all those hats you see on display in the cases and the women buy them. She also makes their hats to order. But many of the women like to make their own. She has all the materials and teaches them. Most of all, they like to remodel their hats. Some of our guests have hats that must be twenty years old; they're constantly having them cleaned and blocked, and giving them a new look with different flowers and feathers and ribbons."

As we moved toward the beauty parlor I thought I glimpsed my friend Mrs. Hancock again, sitting under a dryer.

"This is a busy spot," said Sister, as we looked in the door. "It operates just like any other beauty parlor. We have a professional hairdresser come in, and the women make appointments for their shampoos and hair-dos and permanents. The hairdresser goes up to take care of those who are in bed or who can't come down for one reason or another. Over on the other side we have a fully equipped barber shop for men. They like to keep up appearances, and it does so much for them."

A little old lady waiting for the elevator greeted Sister as we passed. Her silvery hair was beautifully arranged, and topped by a miniature flower garden of a hat.

Sister waited until the elevator had taken her out of hearing distance and then said: "Would you believe that she's a *hundred and one?* And just as spry and interested, one of the liveliest of all our guests. We gave her a big party last year, when she turned a hundred. Come in here, and I'll show you."

She opened a door and snapped on the lights. We entered a studio filled with photographic equipment. Hundreds of photographs covered the walls.

"Here she is," said Sister, pointing to one that showed the little old lady cutting a cake almost as big as she was. I looked at the other pictures of merry parties of old people, couples celebrating anniversaries, guests surrounding famous visitors to the home, performances on the stage in the auditorium, birthday parties.

"Every month," said Sister, "we have a big birthday party, a kind of joint celebration for all the guests who have birthdays during that month. Everybody has a wonderful time. One of our Sisters is a professional photographer, and she's kept busy taking pictures of all that goes on."

We took the elevator upstairs to see the living quarters. We went to the top floor to make it easier to walk down flight by flight. On each floor the elevator opened into a spacious living room with comfortable sofas and chairs, a television set and walls lined with books. Doors opened onto terraces where I could see old folks sunning themselves.

"It makes a comfortable place for the residents of each floor to get together. In fine weather they like to get out of doors and soak up the sunshine. We can't give them a lawn and trees here in the heart of the city, but they like to sit on the terraces. There's always a breeze. They can watch the river traffic, and look out over the city. We have a terrace off the dining room, where they eat in warm weather. Each floor has its own library, too. Our guests can take as many books as they like to their rooms, and keep them as long as they want. And right off the living room on each floor there's a kitchenette."

We looked into the sunny little kitchenette with its stove, sink, refrigerator, and cupboards filled with china and glassware. Sister opened the refrigerator door.

"They keep the foods they like in the refrigerator," she said, "and other snacks, like cookies and crackers, in that cabinet over there."

A counter ran the length of the room, laden with trays and teapots.

"They come in here any time," she explained, "and fix what they like, and take the trays to their rooms. When they have guests it's homey to be able to serve refreshments. Of course, they like taking their guests down to the 'night clubs' and the soda fountain too."

"They're allowed to have guests in their rooms?" I asked.

"Of course!" said Sister, with a faint note of surprise in her voice. "This is their *home*. They can have guests any time, and as late as they want. Naturally, we have to have some rules. For example, visitors can't be so noisy as to disturb other guests, just as in their own homes they wouldn't give parties loud enough to disturb the neighbors."

We walked down the broad corridors, looking into the rooms. All were bright and comfortable, and no two were alike. Most, I noticed, were double rooms with two beds.

"Do you have single rooms?" I asked.

"Oh my, yes," said Sister. "A resident can choose either a single or a double room. And we have a special section of this wing for married couples."

A woman looked out the door of a corner room at the

end of the long corridor. Her face lighted when she saw us.

"Sister!" she called. "A letter came from Jim this morning! Don't you want to read it?"

Sister introduced us, and then she and the woman hugged each other with joy over the arrival of Jim's letter. Sister read it with happy little exclamations, while the woman watched her with shining eyes.

"Jim is her son," Sister explained as we left. "He's a constant visitor, with his family, when he's in this country. But he's been working in South America for the past year."

The elevator door opened, and a cart was rolled out, with dinner trays, stacked in layers, each covered with a starched white napkin.

"Those are for guests who require room service," Sister said. "Of course we encourage all of them to go down to the dining room for meals. But some of them must have meals brought to them, though they're not sick enough to be in bed."

"That's one thing I've been wondering about all morning," I said. "All the old people I've seen are busy and bustling about and happy as teen-agers. Certainly there must be those who are bedridden, and those who have various ailments that require treatment. Where are they? And where are all the wheelchairs I expected to find?"

Sister laughed. "We have plenty of wheelchairs," she said, "and most of them are drawn up to the tables in the dining room right now. Some of our most active guests whip along in wheelchairs—there's no holding them back. You'll notice how wide all the doorways are, and that they have no sills so that wheelchairs can roll right through. But as far as bedridden patients go, and those who require treatment of various kinds, we have a whole wing devoted to them. You've seen only half of the home, the half devoted to ordinary living and recreation. I wanted you to see, first, how truly at home our guests are. Now we'll go into the other wing, and you'll see the kind of care they get."

We knelt for a few minutes in the chapel on our way from one wing to the other. A few of the busy Sisters were kneeling there, renewing their strength at its Source. A dozen or two old people were there too, some kneeling, some sitting quietly.

"I'm going to take you first," said Sister, as we left the chapel, "to our Department of Physical Medicine and Rehabilitation. You've heard a lot about how much longer people are living today. Generally speaking, our lengthened life expectancy is attributed to improved medical care and the new 'wonder' drugs. But rehabilitation is another very important phase of geriatrics. It has been defined by the National Council on Rehabilitation as the restoration of the handicapped to the fullest physical, mental, social, vocational and economic usefulness of which they are capable. It often makes the difference between simple existence and active, happy living."

She explained that residents are given, on admission, a complete physical examination by the physician, who then refers them to the physiatrist. If they can be helped a program of rehabilitation is mapped out, and a course of training or retraining planned for them. A Board of Consultants, made up of specialists in all fields of medicine, is ready to be called in when problems arise.

The object of the program is to produce happy, self-sufficient older people whose general health is at the highest possible level, and whose disabilities are reduced to a minimum. To this end one or several functions of the department may be prescribed for each individual: physical therapy, corrective speech, activities of daily living, occupational and recreational therapy, social service and the like.

"A mistake most older people make," Sister told me, "is

not getting sufficient exercise each day. It's so important, in order to keep muscles and joints flexible. Age seems to bring a natural disinclination to exercise. Of course some old people are over-conscientious about it and tire themselves out. Over-exertion should not be permitted. But the majority who don't exercise are abetted by their relatives and friends, who insist that older people should do nothing but rest. The result, too often, is muscle atrophy, general weakness and lack of balance and coordination."

Each resident, she explained, has an individually pre-scribed program worked out according to his or her specific needs, and treatment is continued even though progress may be slow and, in some cases, a complete cure impossible. Patients with hip fractures, cardiac cases, arthritics, hemi-plegics, diabetics, amputees and parkinsonians may be sent to any or all areas of the rehabilitation program. Many old people come to the home because they are unable to live alone and cannot take care of their personal needs. Some who come directly from hospitals, having been discharged as no longer needing hospitalization, find that they are un-able to return to the special hazards and hardships of living alone or with families who cannot give them the care they need.

We went into the geriatric gymnasium where I saw steps, curbs and stairs to aid old people to walk and to help build their self-confidence. There were adjustable parallel bars, and pulleys.

"We use mat exercises to develop their skill, strength and balance," said Sister, "and pulley exercises to prevent de-formities."

In the physical medicine room there were cubicles con-taining treatment tables, and whirlpool baths to relieve pain and local swelling in the extremities.

"All treatments are prescribed by the physiatrist," Sister

said, pointing out the infra-red heat lamps, cold quartz lamps and low tension machines. "Diathermy is used to bring about relaxation where spasticity is present, to relieve pain and to improve circulation."

"How do the old folks take to their rehabilitation programs?" I asked.

"Beautifully—that is most of them do," Sister answered. "Sometimes it takes a while with newcomers. You see, one of the biggest problems in rehabilitation is that of motivation. We've got to keep encouraging our disabled residents who are under treatment. We must convince them that they can really be helped if they help themselves. We find that most of them are optimistic and try to help themselves. We find, too, that handicapped people are a great source of encouragement to each other. That's why we have the treatment rooms close together in the same area. Actually, most of our guests look forward to their rehabilitation treatments as social get-togethers, a time when they can meet their friends, check up on their mutual progress, and form new contacts with people of their own age who share their own interests."

We passed a door lettered A.D.L.

"Activities of Daily Living," interpreted Sister. "Let's go in; I think this will interest you."

Inside was a homelike living-bedroom with bath.

"All through the house," she explained, "residents are encouraged to do all they possibly can for themselves: combing their hair, washing themselves, getting dressed, taking care of their bathroom needs, feeding themselves and the like. To those who are suffering from a disease or disability that makes such self-care difficult, the retraining they get in here can make the difference between being helpless and being independent."

I looked around. There was a bed, different kinds of

chairs and lamps, a vanity table and other furnishings one would find in an average room.

"For example," Sister went on, "residents are taught to get in and out of bed by themselves, and to transfer from bed to wheelchair and back again."

She pointed to a board on which a number of familiar objects were hanging, each attached to a long stick. One stick had a shoe horn taped to its end, another a wooden scissors-like device for picking up dropped articles. I was puzzled by a spring clothespin attached to one of the sticks.

"That's for putting on socks," explained Sister. "A man who cannot bend over simply clips the back of a sock to the clothespin, and pulls it on his foot. We have all sorts of self-help devices and appliances in here to make sure of adequate performance, but we discourage dependence upon them. Sometimes patients rely too much upon devices and are satisfied to stay at a level below capacity. Of course, all the training given here is part of the patient's individually prescribed program and is geared to his own specific disability. These activities of daily living may seem like little things to a well person but they are most important to the handicapped. Once he has mastered them he is on his way to independent happy living."

There was something familiar about the place, though I had never before been in an A.D.L. room equipped to train old people in this way. I seemed to recognize the different-sized chairs, the little stools and steps, and especially the board with its long sticks holding familiar objects. Then it came to me—I had seen similar rooms, and similar equipment, to train children in the activities of daily living! Children, too, had over-sized equipment: big scissors and clips and clothespins to teach skill and coordination to fumbling little fingers. And now the old people, who had become as little children again to enter Heaven, were being retaught these same activities and skills. How close are the two ends of life!

"Does this kind of retraining take long?" I asked.

"It varies widely, according to the patient," said Sister. "Some can be retrained quickly, and others take a long time. Some can never be fully retrained. But, in general, the results are gratifying, and many are able to leave."

"Are most patients happy to leave?" I asked.

"Oh, no," said Sister. "There are so many stories I could tell you! One that I specially like is about an old man who is one of our guests. He has several married children who were not able to take care of him. I don't know what they thought a 'home for the aged' would be like, but despite the fact that it was the only solution, and that coming here was the old man's own choice, they felt a little guilty, as if in some way they had rejected him. Well, you've never seen such a happy old man. He went along with his prescribed program eagerly, and entered into our activities with enthusiasm. It wasn't long before we made him sacristan in our chapel. When Christmas came his children felt they must have him home for the day. None of them really had a large enough place for the whole family to get together, but they managed to borrow chairs and dishes and a big table and all the rest and planned a celebration, thinking how delighted 'poor old Dad' would be. But 'poor old Dad' had other plans. When they came to invite him he gently refused. 'Too busy,' he told them. 'I'm sacristan now, and Christmas is a busy time in the chapel. I wouldn't miss it for anything. Thanks just the same.' Later he told us, 'This was the happiest Christmas I can ever remember. This is home to me.'"

We went upstairs to the nursing floors, and walked through the women's section, stopping to chat with a number of the patients. The rooms were sunny and glowing with color. The women looked delicate as Dresden dolls, an impression that was heightened by the little ribbon bows they wore in their hair and their frilly lace-ruffled nightgowns. Each was resting on a small pillow, placed on top of the regulation hospital pillow, which had a pretty embroidered case.

"They look like pampered millionaires!" I whispered to Sister.

She laughed. "They're very far from being millionaires but they *are* pampered. We see to that. Pampering is good for them, and you can see how happy they are as a result. You yourself may not like being pampered when you are well, and you may not be the type for pretty, frilly nightgowns and bedclothes. But when you are sick in bed, you love them. Looking pretty and feeling pampered do wonderful things for your morale."

She opened the door of a big closet in the hall and I saw rows of pretty nightgowns and bed jackets hanging inside, each different and all expensive looking.

"We ask for these especially," she explained. "There's not a week that a few don't come in from generous people. Some of these are brand new. They come from expensive shops and must have cost a good deal. Others have been worn but have been so carefully repaired and laundered that they look like new. We have a closet like this on each floor. When a woman becomes bedridden we dress her like a queen. You'd be amazed at the difference it makes."

I thought of the difference as we went on through the occupational therapy department, and as I looked at all the types of work laid out to exercise aging muscles and restore coordination and skill to stiffened hands: knitting, crocheting, sewing, weaving, leather work, clay modeling, metal work, carpentry, and a complete little studio with a window-wall facing north to give proper light for painting.

The difference, I thought, was not simply in facilities and equipment but in love. And love is proved in little things.

The home I went through is one of the finest homes for the aged in the country. Its facilities and equipment are the most modern and complete. I found them overwhelming and, not being an expert, I could not understand all of them. But I could understand the little things.

The big things are necessary: the whirlpool baths and treatment tables, the machines and the therapy rooms, the gymnasium and the A.D.L. equipment, the comfortable bedrooms and cheerful nursing rooms, the dining rooms and the big kitchens, the auditorium and the facilities for entertainment, and the chapel which lies at the heart of it all. Given the wisdom and the money, these things are provided.

But the Sisters know that more than wisdom and money is necessary. Old people need love, and the Sisters' love proves itself in an outpouring of little things. A doctor, a psychiatrist or a social worker would have been tremendously impressed with the big things. I, who am none of these, kept remembering the little things: the perky pink and blue bows on the old women who lay in bed and the embroidered pillowcases under their heads, the closet full of pretty night clothes, the little millinery shop where the women could keep their hats fresh and fashionable through a decade or more of happy wear, the beauty parlor, the soda shop with its busy fountain, Mrs. Hancock bringing in a tray of refreshments from the kitchenette down the hall and entertaining her guests "just like home."

I thought back to that long-ago home for the aged, and remembered the old people sitting, hopeless and forlorn, on rows of bare benches. Even today old people may be filling bare benches in a bare and barren room in some homes for the aged. Many homes are sadly lacking in facilities, and many are overcrowded. Some homes insist upon separating married couples. Others take pride in their facilities and give conscientious care but give it coldly.

But where there are Sisters, there is always love—and love can accomplish wonders even with a minimum of facilities.

As I left the home I turned to Sister.

"I'm tempted to make a reservation for myself right now," I said.

She laughed. "I'm afraid you have a long way to go," she said. "Residents must be at least sixty-five at the time of admission. Actually, the average age of our guests is seventy-eight. We have a long waiting list."

"Supposing one were eligible," I asked, "about how long would one stay on the waiting list?"

"That depends upon individual circumstances," she answered. "A person might have been on the waiting list for two years, and yet we might admit someone who had applied only a few months ago if he had a greater need—if, for example, he were about to be discharged from a hospital and were not able to return home."

"How often do openings occur?"

"Not too often," she said. "Our guests just don't like to leave. They came here of their own choice, and they want to stay. It is important to understand that no one can be 'put' here. Old people must come here themselves, be shown through the place and have everything explained to them. Then they are sent home to think it over. When they come to live here it is their own decision entirely. Once here they are completely 'at home.' They can go off for visits, weekends, vacations, long stays when they like. And they can leave for good, when they wish. But they seldom do. They stay on and on, so naturally our waiting list must be a patient one. We accept all creeds. As a matter of fact, some of our aged Jewish guests can speak nothing but Yiddish, but we have enough Jewish guests who understand them and interpret for us so that there is no language barrier. And there are no financial barriers here either. Some of our guests are well off, some have modest incomes, some have none. God loves them all."

It is because God loves them all that the Sisters love them all. It is the difference that makes all the difference.

X

Stitch in Time

M<small>Y FRIEND</small> Helen has just turned forty, although she insists that she is going to be thirty-nine from here on in.

There seems to be some magic about thirty-nine to which people cling, as if once over the threshold of the forties all hope is gone. I have always thought that if one wishes to set an "ideal" age and refuse (at least in public) to go beyond it, she should set twenty-five, or perhaps thirty, and try to keep physically and emotionally at that level. She would not fool anybody, of course, any more than she fools them at "thirty-nine," but she would be a lot more fun to them and to herself. If I were to set a stopping place for myself, I think it would be short of the brink rather than on top of it. But I am glad I did not stop there. You cannot see the fun and the satisfactions of the forties if you stop short, and the fifties are even better to be in. I have the feeling that the sixties and seventies and beyond will be still better if we know how to use them.

Helen, to her vast surprise, has just had her first brush with geriatrics. A neighbor of hers who had had a new baby asked Helen if she could recommend a good pediatrician. Helen, whose youngest is twelve, had had an excellent pediatrician for her children and recommended him enthusiastically. The proud new mother called him and shortly afterward came knocking on Helen's door.

"Guess what your wonderful Dr. Smith is doing now!" she said, laughing.

Helen who had not had occasion to call Dr. Smith for many years could not imagine.

"He's not taking care of babies any more," her neighbor said, "he's specializing in *old people* now!"

Helen was surprised enough to telephone Dr. Smith.

"Yes," said the doctor, and she could hear him chuckle, "we all grow up. Pediatricians grow up into geriatrists. When you have time, why don't you stop at the office? I'll tell you the story, and perhaps some interesting things about our work. Bring your husband along. It won't be an official visit, just a chat."

Helen and her husband went to see him, then told me about it.

About ten years ago, after a number of years as a successful pediatrician, Dr. Smith turned to geriatrics. He was not alone in changing his field, he said, pointing out that a number of established doctors have recently turned to geriatrics, and that their work is being aided by the many new doctors who train specifically for that field each year.

His ten years in geriatrics have been both interesting and challenging. Although he keeps busy with the health problems of the aged, surprisingly enough most of his patients are in their thirties and forties.

"If we can only make people realize," he said, "that the diseases of old age start in middle life and even before. A person doesn't suddenly go to pieces, so to speak, in old age. If he does, it's because he didn't mend the tiny cracks and bolster the little weaknesses that started showing up in his young adult or middle years. A geriatrist's job is not just to patch up old people and keep them alive and comfortable as long as possible. We try to assure succeeding generations of healthy old people, by starting early enough to be sure they'll be healthy when the time comes."

Dr. Smith's young and middle-aged patients come to him twice a year for a thorough examination, during which the doctor not only looks for disease but also measures their health capacities. The results of each examination are carefully noted down, so that the following examination will reveal even the slightest deviations. In this way he can detect the early beginnings of disease, organic malfunction and degenerative processes.

Helen and her husband have already had their first examination and plan to return regularly.

"Most realistic, common-sense program I know of," her husband says. "It's putting the old principle into practice —paying the doctor to keep you well. It really pays off."

I think the reason that many of us put off taking such positive action to insure a healthy old age is our feeling that old age is a special period that is somehow bracketed off from the rest of life, instead of being a part (and not too well defined a part, at that) of our continuing process of growth.

It is as unrealistic to treat each illness, whether of youth, the middle years or old age, as a phenomenon unrelated to the whole of life, as it is to treat symptoms alone. It is like trying to cure an undue craving for sweets by hiding the candy instead of looking for the underlying cause.

Most of the health precautions we take with our children are forward-looking precautions. We give them inoculations so that they will not be subject to certain illnesses, fortify them with vitamins so they will grow strong and straight, are quick to detect and treat the first symptoms of sight or hearing deficiency, keep even their baby teeth properly cared for, balance their meals conscientiously, and insist upon proper amounts of sleep, play and fresh air. We do not wait until they are obviously in need of such care. We give it to healthy children so that they will grow into healthy adults. And we who have become healthy adults still need regular care so that we will grow into healthy old people.

Of course we do not have to go to a geriatrist nor feel discouraged if there is no such specialist near us. All good doctors are alert these days to the health problems of the aging and to preventive measures in earlier years, just as they keep abreast of the continuing developments and discoveries in the fields of gerontology and geriatrics.

Actually, our family doctor may be best of all for us, because he knows us and our past history so well. My own family doctor, who is as conservative a man as you are likely to meet, knows he has to use "alarmist" tactics with me. When he wants me to stay in bed, or in the house, he warns me of the dire results of going out.

"If you set foot out of this house," he'll say, "I will not be responsible. You're apt to have a setback and be in bed for weeks. No telling what will happen."

If it were anyone else he might say, as any other doctor might say to me under the same circumstances: "Better plan to stay indoors for a while."

But my doctor knows that such a suggestion might keep me indoors for all of five minutes. He once admitted why he tries to scare me.

"I know you and your schedule," he said. "The only thing that could ever keep you indoors would be your own positive conviction that you would fall flat on your face before you'd gone three steps."

Among the best friends we can have during our middle years are doctors who know us well: family doctors, specialists, dentists, oculists. It is up to us to make sure that they know us well, by means of regular and frequent visits.

Perhaps for our own good more doctors should attempt to scare those of us who feel so well during our middle years. We tend to take their suggestions lightly, knowing how many birthdays we can count, and feeling that there is plenty of time ahead during which we can take their advice if we feel we need it. But doctors know that chronological age is not so important as physiological age, and that some organs in our body may be much "older" than we think of ourselves as being. We know that no two of us age at the same rate. Biologically, functionally and mentally, some of us are young at seventy-five; others are old before they reach fifty. But what we seldom realize is that no one of us ages at an even pace. Parts of us may start deteriorating long before other parts and long before we begin to think of ourselves as aging.

Chronic disease is the greatest threat to the aged. As one doctor recently pointed out, we now survive the infectious diseases that once carried off millions of children and young people, but we survive to face the chronic degenerative diseases of old age. Much can be done to prevent such diseases if we start early enough, and much is being discovered and done constantly to help those who suffer from them.

Medical science knows a great deal more about the diseases of the aged than it did ten years ago, or even five years ago. It knows, for example, that the cardiovascular diseases (heart and circulation), cancer, arthritis, and mental disorders, so common among old people, have their beginnings early in life, when they can be detected and cured or controlled.

Do the cardiovascular diseases of old age seem remote to us? It is wise to remember that they, like ulcers, have at least part of their beginnings in the worry, overwork, and emotional tensions that hurry and harry our young and middle years. When the doctor says "Better slow down," he is not simply making conversation.

Do mental disorders seem foreign to us? Think of them the next time you start feeling sorry for yourself and slip into a moody "blue" spell. Depression is a beginning symptom of the mental disorders of old people. It is the first curving of our lives inward upon ourselves, the first attempt to shut out the world and focus our attention and our sympathies upon our own complaints. Many things tempt us, as the years mount, to this unhealthy focusing: imaginary ills as well as very real ones; the forced slowing of our activities; the menopause in women and its equivalent in men; changes in family, social and business life; the thinning out of our contemporaries.

Depression is a disease of the spirit which can lead to disease of the mind. Before it reaches that point, however, it can be cured by spiritual means. Since it is an outgrowth of selfishness, it can be dispelled by a deliberate turning upward and outward. Love of God and, through Him, love of our friends and neighbors and interest in all their concerns leaves no room for selfishness and consequent depression, and does away with the threat of mental disorders stemming from this primary cause.

How about "middle-age spread?" Extra pounds are not serious so long as you keep watching for them and trimming them off before they can accumulate. They become serious when you develop a "what's the use?" feeling, hide the scales in the closet, and take to consoling yourself for disappointments with snacks and sundaes.

I do not suppose that upon meeting a fat person for the first time, any of us would immediately conclude from his size that he is a "spiritual" person. A fat person may indeed be holy, but halos are not hung on him according to how he tips the scales. Yet there is a deeper connection between the spirit and obesity than many people imagine; so much so that obesity, so common among the aged, may be called a spiritual ill because it stems, in most cases, from an illness of the spirit.

Some old people lose their appetites, and must be retrained in good eating habits. But many try to find in food compensation for spiritual ills: loneliness, disappointments, bereavement, loss of a physical faculty, lack of love, unpleasant surroundings, poverty, the aging process itself with its limitations. As one pleasure after another slips from their grasp or fades as it must with the years, food remains as a constant pleasure and they seize upon it. Often their preoccupation with food becomes their only pleasure. It is significant that, like children, such people have no interest in a balanced diet, but seek the rich and starchy foods that they find so "consoling."

During the same period when they eat heavily (and more unwisely), their activities become, of necessity, limited. They sit more and spread as they sit. They do not get around as much as they used to, if at all. They are disinclined to exercise or perhaps unable to. They are unhappy people and so they eat. The more they eat, the fatter they get. As the pounds mount so do their problems. Obesity opens the door to serious diseases in the later years and often closes the door upon its victims before they even reach those years.

Dieting alone cannot help reduce overweight. Since overweight is, in most cases, a spiritual ill, spiritual motivation must put the diet to work and keep it operating. We must seek the reason for our compulsive eating, and realize how absurd we are to suppose that eating will correct the condition or restore the loss that set us off on our calorie stuffing. We must cultivate other interests besides food, and in them find reason to *want* to lose weight.

Does it seem far-fetched to say that prayer melts pounds? It is not far-fetched, though the statement is an over-simplification. You can storm Heaven with prayers for a sylph-like figure without losing an ounce. But if you pray to find the spiritual ill that has led you to an eating compulsion, it will be shown to you. And if you face it with humility and hope, and pray for strength to rise above it, you will find the strength you need flooding you. You will *want* to lose weight, and you will.

It is far better, of course, to be moderate with food as with all else throughout life. It is far easier to stay at our normal weight than to try to regain it, particularly from the middle years on. But if we lose the battle of the bulge, it need be only a temporary defeat if we remember our two sources of help: prayer to enable us to see our spiritual lack and persist in our efforts to overcome it, and a diet carefully tailored to our specific needs by a doctor. Dieting without a doctor's continuing supervision can be as dangerous as obesity itself.

It is interesting to see the constantly greater attention that is being given to the spiritual in modern medicine. There was a time when medicine focused entirely upon the physical and took its eyes off men's bodies only to peer through microscopes and X-ray machines in order to probe our innermost physical secrets. But doctors have come to realize that mental strains, worries and tensions can destroy the human body faster and more effectively than germs, that despite our tremendous discoveries of disease-destroying chemicals, vitamins and "wonder" drugs mental disorders are spiralling, and that more people are reaching their early forties with heart disease, high blood pressure, nervous disorders, ulcers and cancer than ever before in history. You might almost say that disease has kept advancing as swiftly as medical science. Doctors and scientists have had to look beyond men's bodies and recognize the spiritual force that gives them life.

Only if a man's spirit gives him reason for living and the will to live, can medicines help him combat the forces of physical destruction and survive them. Medicine is, for the first time, recognizing the whole man, body and soul, and in doing so has taken its greatest step ahead, as well as giving the greatest promise for its future.

In the rehabilitation of the aged and disabled, for example, spiritual motivation is of first importance. This motivation may be the realization of one's relationship with God, or the wish to be an active and useful member of society once more, or merely the desire to help oneself. In any case it is spiritual, and it arises in the will. A shocking number of old people surrender to disease and are left to rust away in beds or in wheelchairs, because they and their families believe that "old age" itself is a disease and, at best, a waiting for death.

In a recent survey of ninety-five unselected aged patients in New York City municipal hospital wards, it was found that only seven of them needed continued hospitalization, and two of these were questionable. The survey was undertaken by a study group made up of physicians, social workers, psychologists, nurses, occupational and physical therapists and hospital chaplains. They found that of the ninety-five, eighty-four needed no further medical care or rehabilitation. Eleven were held suitable for further training with a fifty per cent prospect of successful rehabilitation. Yet these ninety-five old people had spent a total of more than a quarter of a million days in municipal hospitals! The cost to the city and its taxpayers was staggering, running into millions of dollars. And, as one of the investigating doctors pointed out, the cost in human values, boredom, anxiety, frustration and resignation was incalculable.

Of course the problem does not stop there. Releasing these people, and uncounted numbers like them, to active useful lives in their communities involves community effort, too. Well-organized community rehabilitation centers would carry the work along and prevent the crowding of our hospitals by custodial patients. This in turn would require professionally trained personnel of which there is a critical shortage. It is not work for a few generous volunteers but a vital work for everyone to start and support on community or parish level, in order to relieve present urgent conditions and in order to insure that the situation does not mushroom beyond all control by the time we number ourselves among the aged. Those who are not interested in working for others must be shown that they are, in very truth, working for themselves.

The so-called "religious revival" we have been experiencing during recent years in this country could be a great force for good if teamed with medicine's acceptance of the spiritual as a prime factor for physical health. There are many who challenge the sincerity of our so-called revival, who see much of it as surface-shallow rather than spirit-deep. I believe that it is good even if it is only a first step in the right direction. A man may go to church for no other reason than to be seen there by people he wishes to impress, or may engage in philanthropic work with one eye on the polls in an election year, but God has a way of taking many steps to our one and surprising such a man before he has gone very far.

An instance of medicine's recognition of the needs of the spirit, though without specific reference to religion, is seen in the "programs for living" charted for old people by the geriatric clinic of a great university's medical school. It is located in Florida and is an outstanding example of medicine's broadening scope to include treatment of the whole person.

Admission to the geriatric clinic is limited to those who are sixty-five or over, and who seem to have medical, social or psychological problems that bear on their state of health. The clinic sees itself as a living laboratory for the investigation of the problems of the aged, and defines good health as a state of well-being, not merely the absence of disease. In the words of its directors: "The structure of the Clinic is dictated by the concept that a person is an ego structure, or personality, which resides within a body, and uses this body as a tool with which to make contact with his environment. In this kind of setting the body becomes merely the medium by which the ego structure is enabled to get satisfactions out of the world around him. Although the ego, body and environment must operate as a totality, for purposes of analysis they are naturally studied by a social worker, psychologist and a physician."

We who know that man's purpose is not "to get satisfactions out of the world around him" but rather to know, love and serve God in this world that we may gain the happiness of Heaven will find much to question in the clinic's concept, but we must agree that it is a far cry from the days when old people were given pills for their complaints, told to "stop worrying," and left to rust away!

Each patient at the clinic is seen by a group of specialists, and conferences are held periodically at which all the cases that have been studied adequately are reviewed. To this conference are invited a number of people from the "helping professions" in the community, to help plan a program of living for each patient.

"In this way," the directors say, "the Clinic ties together

in the one setting a number of varied disciplines bearing upon the total adjustment to life of an aged person. We are interested in developing the capacity of the patient to use his medical, psychological, and socio-economic assets in order to find the happiest solution to living. Periodically, reviews are undertaken to see whether or not we have been successful in improving the life situation of these aged people."

Upon arrival at the clinic the patient's chief complaint is noted, a social worker takes down his history, and he is turned over to the examining physician. After a complete physical examination the doctor studies his findings and the patient's history in order to arrive at a proper interpretation: the individual's life expectancy and reasons for it; his physical limitations; specific activities the patient can or cannot do, depending upon whether his limitations are visual, auditory, neuro-muscular or cardiovascular; possible improvement under medical supervision; and expected increase in the patient's limitations, together with the probable period of time it will take to occur.

He is sent next to an examining psychologist who determines his present mental status and his "ego capacity" both to participate in new experiences and to withstand negative experiences. An evaluation is made of his present interests and aptitudes, his capacity to make new friends, the extent of a healthy curiosity in people and activities and events. His capacity to withstand negative experiences is measured in regard to such trials as the death of a mate, narrowing of social contacts, loss of previous useful interests and activities such as employment or hobbies, increase in physical limitations predicted by the examining physician, surgery, hospitalization and institutionalization.

Then the patient returns to the social worker who determines in the light of these findings which community resources are available for the increasing or enriching of the patient's orbit of living. To meet his physical needs he may require a visiting nurse and physician, prosthetic devices, a housekeeper or maid service, transportation, better housing, recreational facilities or financial aid. He may need case work, psychiatric help or group therapy to help him emotionally. On the social side friendly home visiting, group activity or volunteer projects in church or community may be recommended. And for his intellectual needs useful and interesting activities, hobbies or participation in classes may be indicated.

All findings and recommendations are put before the periodic conferences, which use them to map out each patient's individual program for living. It is interesting to note that the "helping professions" in the community participate in the discussions and the programming, because without community awareness of the problem and willingness to take action, the best of programs can be crippled if not rendered ineffectual.

In a recent conference of doctors, a surprising and gratifying human note tempered the usual scientific proceedings —and, according to the best medical thought, belonged there just as much as all the learned talk. The doctors' discussion turned to accidental injuries to the aged, the third most frequent cause of death in people over sixty-five. It was noted that surgery is no longer the risk with old people that it once was, that an old person's chances of recovery from major surgery are good, and that a surgeon must be prompt to operate, if in his judgment it is necessary, even if he must convince a reluctant patient and an unwilling family to accept surgical aid.

The management of an old person after an accident is just as important, the doctors agreed. He must not be allowed to feel that he has come to a full stop, because actually he is no sicker than before his accident. He should be treated as a well person and not loaded down with sympathy nor pestered with everlasting questions as to how he feels. He should be encouraged to carry on every activity possible to him under the circumstances: his work, hobbies and social activities. Exercise of all uninjured parts should be insisted upon from the first day. If he is in the hospital, the doctors were told to try to persuade the dietitian to cater to his idiosyncrasies in food, within the limits, of course, of the hospital diet. If he has smoked most of his life, he should be allowed to go on smoking. If he is accustomed to a nip or two, he should be allowed to "exercise his usual tolerance." And the doctors were warned to keep a watchful eye on the hospital nurses, lest they try to spirit away the red flannel undershirt that some old men insist on wearing!

Accidents can occur to any of us, at any age or any time, although care and reasonable caution will prevent most of them. But many of the ills of old age, certainly those that we dread most, begin in our middle years and earlier. We need only be alert to their beginnings, when it is easy to cure or control them, and to remember that spiritual ills are often at the root of physical ones.

Vigilance is more than the price of liberty; it is the price of health too. And it is what any housewife who knows value would call a bargain price.

XI

———⚬———

The Pattern

ONE of the important advantages of being a mother or a teacher is frequent exposure to the pure truth of children. It is sometimes disconcerting but always refreshing. We so often pile our scales with all manner of things when we attempt to weigh values that we are never quite sure of the validity of our judgments. Children keep their scales free of nonessentials and judge more truly.

A family friend of ours was once weighed in such a children's scale. He had been abroad for several years, and when he returned there was a new member of the family to meet him, my son Robin who was then four. When he left after a pleasant visit, I said to my son:

"How did you like Uncle Jerry?"

Robin considered the matter carefully for several minutes. I could almost see the delicate balancing of the scale. Then he said, with simple assurance:

"I like him better than meat balls."

It was a shining triumph for Jerry. Meat balls were Robin's favorite food, and were not easily surpassed in his affections. I could not have made so true a judgment, and I must admit, though not without shame, that there are more than a few people I like *less* than meat balls.

I remember another son's first trip to the seashore. We

were picnicking on a deserted stretch of beach. Peter could not keep his eyes from the ocean which filled the horizon. He watched the breakers coming in, pounding from far off, and hushing to little ripples on the sand. He stood on tiptoe trying to see beyond the horizon the end of all that water.

"What do you think of the ocean?" his father asked.

"I don't know," said Peter. "There's too much."

"Well, do you like it?" his father persisted.

Peter grabbed his little pail and ran down to the water's edge and filled it. When he came back he put the pail down and squatted beside it. Carefully he dipped a finger into the water in the pail, then licked his finger.

"I like part of it," he said. "It's nice and wet, but it tastes too salty."

A statistician would have called his action, I suppose, an instinctive sort of cross-section analysis. But we do not have to be statisticians to realize that the particular is easier to understand than the general. People in general cannot be understood and loved as people in particular can.

That is why it was so helpful to our understanding of all the generalizations we have been hearing about the aged, to have Catholic Charities let down a sample pail into a quiet little pool of them recently, in St. Louis, and come up with particulars. The sampling was part of an impartial study, directed by Archbishop Ritter of St. Louis, of needs in the area, in order that Catholic organizations and institutions might keep abreast of the times in their thinking and their planning.

The Church has been on the receiving end of the same questions that have been flooding government, state and municipal agencies: What about work opportunities for the aged? Housing facilities? How can people save for their later years? What about health care, family relationships, self-help? Finding answers to these and many more questions is part of the Church's social mission.

In planning the study, it quickly became evident that in order to get a real picture, it would not suffice merely to study institutions and hospitals, because less than four per cent of the thirteen and a half million people over sixty-five in the country are institutionalized. Therefore, to be complete, the study must include the aged and chronically ill in their own homes.

It was decided to focus attention upon a typical parish as a small world that would mirror the constants and the variables of the big one. The parish was chosen carefully. It would not do to study one in an area that was disintegrating, or one that consisted chiefly of upper-middle-income families. The one finally selected, with the whole-hearted cooperation of its pastor, was a parish that had been established in 1920 and that has a considerable lower-middle-income population.

The area the parish covers originally had been parceled off into German dairy farms, and much of the German pattern survives there: the tradition of the large family, the well-defined family solidarity, the deep conviction on the part of the people of their right to work and to participate in the programs of the parish. But there are large Irish and Italian groups too, and a good healthy spicing of the so-called new immigration, the Poles and the Slovaks. Two-thirds of the elderly parishioners interviewed had been born in the United States. All in all, a typical and truly American parish.

As the interviewers made their rounds, they were struck most forcibly by the fierce spirit of independence evident among the old people and their families. Despite hardships and uncertainties, the hazards of a depression period and the ups and downs of health and finances, they had retained their self-respect and independence and were eager to work out their own problems for themselves. With but few exceptions, full cooperation was given to the interviewers, which entailed some patience on the part of those interviewed because the questionnaires were lengthy and detailed and more than half the families were visited from four to six times during the course of the study.

Their findings were broken down under various headings: health, home ownership, work, income and economic security, and religion in the life of the aging.

As the study states, illness that virtually incapacitates people completely and permanently is one of the great challenges confronting the medical profession, the nursing profession, and students of social legislation today. Voluntary agencies, swamped with the problem of chronic illness, are insisting that it is a government responsibility. But the government, although it can build hospitals, cannot staff them because of the critical shortage of personnel, and states are unwilling to use available federal funds for the construction of hospitals for the care of the chronically ill. Time and again, those directing the St. Louis parish study were reminded by leaders in the medical profession that a new assessment of family responsibility in the field of the chronically ill was needed.

They found more of such family responsibility in the parish than had been suspected. Its extent was an important factor in their findings and provided new evidence of family solidarity. The study showed that fifteen per cent of the aged could be classified as chronically ill, and found that these old people were being cared for in their own homes by their own children. There was no thought of shifting responsibility or of asking for outside assistance. In every case the family and neighbors rallied around, and those families whose members went to work made arrangements for chronically ill members to be cared for during the day by practical nurses.

This was the case, for example, with an eighty-six-year-old woman living with her daughter. The mother has been helpless since she had a fall a few years ago, but she faces her problems cheerfully and manages to get around with the aid of a walker. The daughter, who must work for a few more years in order to qualify for a pension, employs a practical nurse to care for her mother during the day.

Another woman of eighty-five, who broke her hip five years ago and was hospitalized for months, lives with her son and daughter-in-law who have paid all her hospital and medical bills. She is lively, alert and interested in all that is going on.

The interviewers were impressed by a little old woman of seventy-three who lives alone and is proud of her independence, although she is totally blind. She does most of her own cooking, cleaning and laundry and her home is spotless. A friendly neighbor visits her each day to help her with some of the work, and the parish priests visit her regularly to her great joy.

Most of the old people who are not chronically ill rated their health as good or fair and took an encouraging attitude toward it. When illness struck, children, relatives, Church and neighbors all pitched in. There were many evidences of neighbors sharing the nursing care and taking over some of the household responsibilities. Interest on the part of pastor and other parish priests, expressed in frequent visits, was given great importance in time of illness.

A surprise factor was the discovery that over half of the older people relied on hospital group insurance to meet the expenses of extended hospital care. The interviewers had not supposed that such insurance had reached any large number of today's old people. Savings and dependence upon relatives accounted for the payment of bills on the part of those who were not insured.

Home ownership was found to be the biggest undertaking and the biggest economic interest of the families interviewed. From the beginning, and through years of difficulty and depression, they had struggled to own and to maintain the homes that were the center of their lives, the symbol of strong family ties, and the only solid security that they could understand. Many homes in the parish have become two- and three-generation homes over the years. It was obvious that the people of the parish were proud of their homes and their well-kept gardens.

"What's the use of owning your own home if you can't make your own repairs?" one man asked. "You wouldn't keep it long if you had to keep paying people to repair it for you."

An interesting example of young people sharing the apostolate of service to others was observed in the numbers of them who joined together on a block-by-block basis to repair the homes and tend the gardens of old people who lived alone.

A surprising number of old people were found to be regularly employed. The attitude of the entire area toward work was a healthy one. The people have a deep sense of the importance of work in their lives, and one of the most frequent subjects of discussion when neighbors meet is the kind of work that may be found after retirement. "Substitute work," they call it.

Some of them have found this substitute work. A retired carpenter does many repair jobs in the neighborhood and in addition has taken over several vacant lots, with the permission of their owners, and sells the vegetables he grows there. A retired fireman is doing painting, carpentry and plumbing for his neighbors. The desire to work was evident even among the physically handicapped, many of whom have developed their own forms of self-employment. A number of the women take in roomers, while others give a good deal of time to personal service on a neighborhood basis.

What kind of income does this cross section of old people have?

The study shows that many of them still rely upon their own earnings or those of a mate for their chief source of support. About a third look to Old Age and Survivors Insurance as their main resource. A sixth depend on children and relatives to support them. Less than a tenth have private pensions. About four per cent rely either upon Old Age Assistance, or upon the income received for renting out a room or apartment.

A fairly constant financial pattern was unearthed by the interviewers. Knowing that these old people had lived as income-producing adults during the depths of the depression years of the thirties, the interviewers questioned them about those years in order to compare their situation then and now.

About half of them are better off now than they were then. About a third are just about in the same position, financially as they were during the depression, and a fifth are worse off. Half of them are comfortably situated today, a little less than half have sufficient to get along on, two per cent are really well to do, and five per cent are not making ends meet at all. What seems to be a continuing pattern is that none of those who are now well off had to seek aid during the thirties, only a small portion of those who are now comfortable economically sought aid then, while a larger proportion of those who cannot now make ends meet had to seek help during the depression years from relatives, charitable groups or the government.

From these findings, it would seem that we carry with us

our economic habits and our attitudes toward earning, thrift
and extravagance, saving and spending, providing for the
future and dependence upon others in a pinch into old age
along with our physical, mental and spiritual characteris-
tics.

One phase of the questioning showed, I think, unusual
perception on the part of those directing the study. The old
people were asked about the resources on which they felt
they should depend during their last years. They were not
asked about the resources on which they were actually
depending, because that had been determined previously.
These questions were, rather, a looking back and a wishful
thinking. They should be helpful to us who are looking
forward to our later years instead of looking back from
them; a kind of hindsight on the part of others which
may spur our own foresight.

"If I had only . . ." can be sad or tragic, depending upon
what it was we neglected to do. Thus, in planning our
own measure of financial security for the day after tomorrow, it is interesting to note that about half of the old people in the parish thought that they should have made pro-
vision for their later years by savings or annuities. About
a quarter of them felt that they should be able to look to
their children for economic support. A slightly smaller number felt that they should be able to look to a contributory
type of government pension like Old Age and Survivors
Insurance or the Railroad Retirement Act, or that there
should be some form of general pension. A few felt they
should have been able to depend on an employer-provided
plan, or a benefit plan based on need.

Things should be a little easier for us when our time comes,
because the problems posed by our lengthening span of
years have been making themselves felt in government, business and industry.

Social Security has already increased its benefits, and expanded them to cover more people in more kinds of employment. Old people can now, for example, earn up to $1,200 a year and still collect their Social Security checks, and of course earn any amount at all after they turn seventy-two without forfeiting them. We may in the future see this resource further increased and expanded. Life insurance companies are working on the possibilities of contracts that will benefit more "overage" policy holders, and companies dealing in health, accident and hospital insurance have become aware of the need for correcting some of their age limitation and cancellation clauses. Many businesses are reviewing the kind of pensions they have been paying, under which retired employees get certain fixed payments, with the idea of making such pensions more realistic and helpful by tying them in with the cost of living.

There are more and more counselors, working independently and through business personnel offices and banks, to advise people approaching retirement and to help them map out economic programs for the years ahead. Books and pamphlets on every aspect of planning for security in the later years are flooding the market. Books, of course, can do little more than deal in generalities when it comes to financial matters, because each person's circumstances are so highly individual, but they can point out where more specific help can be obtained. With all the help available to us, we should have no need some day to say "If I had only . . ."

The Church, according to the St. Louis parish study, occupies an important place in the lives of the old people. They have a deep feeling about the importance of their membership in such a vital institution, and their strong religious convictions find expression in the sacrifices, all too often heroic, that are necessary in their care of the chronically ill, as well as in the neighborly personal service going on in every block of the area. This block-by-block service makes no distinction between class or creed, and is a fine spontaneous neighborly service that is unencumbered by machinery, reports or statistics. It is warm and freely given, and more significant than its simplicity would indicate.

Most of the old people want to maintain their active participation in the affairs of the parish. Some, of course, are not able to get around, but most of those who have dropped out of parish activities said it was because they do not like night meetings. More older women than men were continuing to participate, pointing out that women's organizations usually meet during the day.

When the older people were asked for suggestions as to the activities they would like to see their parish church promote for them, friendly visiting by parishioners was put at the top of the list. The study sees such personal service as basic in the life of the Church, and suggests that the Church's great contribution to the service of the aged, the blind, the chronically ill and shut-ins may well be on a neighborhood block basis.

Next in importance to friendly visiting, the old people asked for religious and recreational programs, not specifically for their own age group but parish-wide activities in which they might participate. Many of them also suggested an organized method of arranging transportation for those who are unable to get to church by themselves.

"We cannot deal with the place of religion and the Church in the life of the aging," the study reports, "without taking into account the general outlook and attitude toward life's basic problems. On the whole, the aging had an objective outlook on life. They did not pass their days in worrying about the future or the past. Their convictions about life and its purpose were truly Christian. They were not too much concerned about death. They looked at it from a Christian standpoint. They recognized that their lives, even at best, were relatively short. They want to continue their activities. They want to continue in constructive work. They want to continue their active participation in the affairs of their families, of their children and grandchildren.

"This is one of the great lessons we learned; it gave us a new vision of the place the large family still occupies in our lives. From the participation in large family reunions we found that, on the whole, the aging in the parish were living in the new age, not of the patriarchal or matriarchal family, but of the democratic, Christian family. They did not give us the impression that they wanted to pattern their children or their grandchildren. They wanted the children of the new generation to do their own thinking and their own planning in the light of the new problems confronting them.

"The aging in the parish do not present many problems that they themselves and their families cannot solve through their own efforts, or with the ordinary aids that are at their disposal through the growing Social Security program, through private pensions of one kind or another, and through the various health and hospital benefits that are available in the community on an increasingly large scale. This satisfactory state of life can be seen in their description of their lives. More than half described their life as generally happy, about half regarded it as average, and about one person in fifty described his past life as unhappy."

A study such as was made in this parish is by no means a definitive survey of the aged in general, as those who made it would be first to agree. It was so carefully and thoroughly conducted and analyzed by experienced people, however, that it is at least an accurate picture of old people in that particular parish. Plans are being discussed now for studying other types of parishes in the same way, so that little by little the picture will grow, and with it knowledge that we can apply to over-all as well as particular problems.

But even in this single parish study, a pattern begins to emerge that seems to be basic enough to show up in further studies.

Income levels may differ, as well as hopes and aspirations, and there are sure to be sharp differences between big-city, small-town and country groups. We will not find the comforting security of home ownership in city parishes made up of apartment houses and tenements. But knowing that the wish for such security is deep in the hearts of old people, who knew homes in their youth, will help us find other means of providing a basic sort of security for them.

And we will almost surely not find the neighborly service that was so important a factor in the St. Louis parish study in large sections of our big cities. But seeing its importance sharply etched as these studies continue, we will be impelled to go knocking on our neighbors' doors and doing for them what they are not able to do for themselves.

New? No newer than the Golden Rule. Our every discovery about the needs of our neighbors and our responsibilities toward them was taught us, long ago, by a Man Who loved them so much He died for them.

XII

—— ·•· ——

The One Thing Necessary

WE HAD A BIG FUNERAL, as funerals go, in our parish a few weeks ago. The woman who died was not a celebrity but she had been a good woman and a good parishioner and the church was full.

She had been a cheerful and active parishioner ever since she moved here years ago as a young bride. For years she had been a working pillar of the Rosary Society. For years she had met with the Helping Hand group on Wednesday afternoons to make bandages for the cancerous poor. How many miles of bandages she rolled and how many mountains of pads she folded so carefully nobody knows, but everybody can guess how much love was rolled up with the bandages and how many prayers were folded into the pads.

Then she was not seen around any more. There were rumors, and whispers of "cancer," and head-shaking. When she died, it was a moving tribute to see the entire Rosary Society assemble at the wake and recite the Rosary.

I met one of her daughters last week. "Such a beautiful funeral," I said, "and wasn't it wonderful how all the women turned out to say the Rosary. It showed what they thought of her."

"Did it?" she asked, with a touch of bitterness. "Mother

could have used a little of that thoughtfulness before she died."

She spoke hesitantly at first, but then some sort of compulsion sent her words tumbling out. I could tell that they had been too long held back.

"Mother was sick for seven months," she said. "She was in the hospital for a month, and they sent her home to die because they couldn't do anything for her. The cancer was too far advanced. So she lay in bed for six whole months but not one of those women so much as stopped in to see her. Father's visits were her only bright spots. He'd come in every week, and bring her Communion; but he's a busy man, and you can't expect him to sit and talk for an hour. You can't imagine what those long days were like, with the clock hardly moving. At the beginning she used to listen for the doorbell, but she never said anything until near the end. 'I guess the women have been busy,' she said. That was all. Those busy bandage-makers and their cancerous poor—couldn't a couple of them have come over and made their bandages beside the bed of one of their own who was dying of cancer?

"Yes, it was an impressive turnout the Rosary Society made at the wake. Don't think we didn't appreciate it. But instead of all of them spending that hour together there, if they had taken turns and each spent an hour with Mother during her illness, she could have had a friendly caller every day of those six months. Maybe she would have lived longer, who knows? At any rate, she would have lived and died more happily."

Our parish is a big city parish. Maybe it is different in small-town and country parishes, where the corporal works of mercy have not yet been organized out of existence, where one person's need is still everybody's business, and where neighborly concern is not yet considered nosiness.

It would, of course, be foolish to make a sweeping indictment of city parishes. It would not be fair, for one thing, because there is an anonymous core of living, breathing, working saints in each of them. And it would not be fair, for another thing, because their accomplishments are too big to measure. What big city parishes have done and are doing in terms of Catholic education, youth programs, social welfare, civic betterment, support of the Church in her seminaries, charities, missions could not be accomplished on such a scale by small-town and country parishes.

But something has gone wrong somewhere. Something has gone very wrong when Mrs. Jones can die through six months of lonely days and nights because "the women are busy," when little Mrs. Smith can worry herself into jumping nerves and crying jags because she does not know what to do with her three little ones while she goes to the hospital for her fourth; when old Mrs. Brown sits forlorn and forgotten at her window Sunday mornings because the family has no car and she can no longer walk to Mass; and when Grandpa Green has taken to talking to himself because there is nobody else to talk to.

I think it is because we in the cities have become so busy about so many things that we have forgotten the one thing necessary. There are so many demands upon us, and they set up such a clamor, that they all seem necessary. So, like big business, we become efficient. We organize and specialize and delegate. We hold meetings and serve on committees and conduct drives. Our intentions are good and our causes are worthy, but by some strange alchemy we ourselves become a little less good and a little less worthy. Perhaps it is because we become a little less human.

We big-city people are big-hearted people. Let someone
in need be written up in the papers and we cannot do enough
for him. We are pushovers for publicity. An old couple is
threatened with eviction and offers of money and jobs and
living quarters pour in. We rush to donate our blood to a
stranger when an appeal is sent out. An old man's wheelchair is stolen, the judge blasts the thief as the "meanest
man in the world," and next day a dozen wheelchairs arrive at the old man's door. An aging music teacher needs
a piano if she is to continue to give lessons to support herself and her phone keeps ringing all day with offers. In New
York each Christmas, the *Times* publishes its accounts of
the city's hundred neediest cases and we empty our pockets—while the hundreds of needy cases in our own parish
are overlooked.

We may be thoughtless but we are not selfish people. We
are softies—soft-hearted and soft-headed. We have lost our
sense of order and balance, and we have confused sentiment
with charity. We consider ourselves neighbors to the world,
when actually we have forgotten how to be neighbors to the
people next door.

The old people reported on in the St. Louis parish study
told the interviewers that what they needed and wanted
most was friendly visiting. It was not a surprise request,
but a need that welfare organizations have long been
aware of. "Friendly visiting" as a term with specific measur-
able meaning has become a familiar part of the vocabulary
of these organizations.

I was talking not long ago about the needs of the aging
with one of the directors of this work for the New York
Catholic Charities. I asked him what he considered their
greatest need.

"Friendly visiting," he said, without hesitation.

I must have looked surprised, because I had been studying so many of the problems of the aged, and had discovered so many pressing needs. Friendly visiting seemed such a casual kind of thing to be placed at the top of the list.

He noticed my reaction and smiled.

"There it is, quite simply," he said. "Right now our greatest need is for friendly visiting. This is not to minimize our other needs. We have many of them, and they are important. We need constructive programming and legislation to help along all fronts in our dealings with the problems of the aging. We need to alert the public to their problems, to re-emphasize the obligation of children toward aging parents, and to enable more of the aged, with certain supportive helps, to stay in their own homes. More day-care centers are needed. Nursing and homemaker services for the chronically ill or incapacitated aged in their own homes must be greatly expanded; a particularly acute aspect of the problem is the hard core of aging who are in need of nursing care. Free medical service is available now only to those living on Old Age Assistance, but we are hoping to see it expanded to cover those with Social Security or perhaps with a small pension; in other words, those who have enough money to exclude them at present from such free care, yet not enough money to be able to afford to pay for medical care.

"And another of our big problems is housing. Old people who live alone—and the greater number of our old people here in the city live alone—meet with an accident, such as a fall, and go to the hospital. But the hospitals can't keep them indefinitely, and as soon as they no longer require hospitalization they are discharged. Where can they go? They are not yet able to take care of themselves. They are not ready or able to live alone as they did before. But they could go home if they had nursing service, homemaker care and friendly visiting. So you see, it all ties in together. Nursing is a professional service, and homemaker service requires certain training. But friendly visiting requires only love of God and good will."

He told me that the only organized friendly visiting on the part of lay people in New York now, aside from the friendly aspects of the more specialized kind of visiting by the Legion of Mary, the St. Vincent de Paul Society and welfare workers, is done by the Ladies of Charity. There are only about a thousand of them in the New York Archdiocese, and they operate, as they must, on a parish level. When a call comes to Catholic Charities from an aged person needing this kind of assistance, the central office of the Ladies of Charity is alerted. They find out which parish the aged person lives in, then get in touch with a Lady of Charity in that parish who visits the old man or woman.

Their work is good and sorely needed. They are generous, dedicated and self-sacrificing women. But the flaws in the system are obvious even to them. In the first place, there are not nearly enough of them, and certainly not one of them in every parish, nor even in the majority of parishes. In the second place, few aged people, however much they might like someone to visit them, actually call and ask. Members of their families or neighbors seeing their need are apt to call for medical care, nursing care, or homemaker service but seldom for a friendly visitor. For every call that comes in, there are thousands of old people who spend their days in silent solitude.

Service like this cannot be organized from without, but must flow out from within. It is a matter of conscience, of the charity to which we are commanded. It is a project no bigger than our own parish, our own neighborhood, our own block, our own hearts. Yet it can change our present and shape our future.

Yes, organization is often necessary, because of our numbers today. Officers and committees and minutes and reports are necessary because so many of us must be directed and shown where and how to help. We have raised our sights to citywide, statewide, national and international levels; now we must adjust them again to our own streets. We have become so occupied with Church affairs on a diocesan and national and worldwide level, that we tend to forget that the Church is only as healthy as each of her parishes is healthy. What a difference it would make if we Catholics started spelling Catholic Action with small letters: *catholic action.* If we took it out of committee and made it personal, down to earth, grass-roots, urgent.

To function effectively and to be truly helpful, friendly visiting must operate on the parish level and preferably on the block level within the parish. It cannot be institutionalized and yet some sort of organization or supervision is indicated in order that people in need be searched out, contacts maintained and further help secured when necessary.

Since the publicizing of the need for friendly visiting in the St. Louis report, many people have asked those conducting the study how such personal service can be extended without institutionalizing it.

"This," they reply, "is the eternal question. How can we get the highest expression of Christian brotherhood, the type described in the Sermon on the Mount and in St. Paul's Epistle to the Corinthians, without institutionalizing it? People keep asking us how far existing organizations can promote this neighborly service without stereotyping it. One thing is sure, they cannot promote it by some of our present highly specialized and mechanized methods."

But there are existing organizations tailor-made for this

important parish-level work: parish societies. If our parish societies made the corporal works of mercy the first of their projects, it would transform both the societies and the parish. If, for example, each meeting opened with a short prayer for guidance, followed by a ten-minute period of silence during which each member would think—not of the approaching card party or of the raffle to help the unwed mothers of Calcutta—but of everybody in the parish who needs help of some kind, a change would soon be apparent. They might recall the sick people, convalescents, the aged, old people who live alone, the newly bereaved, overworked mothers, homes where a little neighborly help is needed, newcomers to the parish and converts who feel strange and a little lost.

They might remember the people who need to be driven to Mass or to the doctor or the clinic, expectant mothers who need help in the home while they're in the hospital, people who need a baby-sitting break but cannot pay for it, people to whom it would be a godsend to be able to borrow baby clothes or a crib or a carriage or, at the other end of life, a wheelchair or a radio or a few warm blankets. It would be a fruitful ten minutes indeed if every member reported every case that came to mind (remembering that the parish embraces everybody within its boundaries, Catholic and non-Catholic, just as Christ's love embraces them), and if volunteers were assigned to follow each case faithfully during the month and to report at the next meeting.

The help given would be a double blessing, because it would not only help those in need of friendly visiting, but it would help the visitors too. Old people in the parish who are active and able to get around, who may themselves be members of the parish societies, would blossom under the responsibility of such assignments and the knowledge that they are needed for such important work. There is a great deal of it that they are especially fitted to do. They have more time to do it than those of us who must go to work or keep busy with home and children. They are eager to do it and need only be told how and where.

But we others cannot be absolved of personal responsibility in the matter by delegating the work to the active aged. Those in need on our block are our responsibility whether or not we belong to a parish society or, if we do, whether or not our parish society decides to make the corporal works of mercy in general, and friendly visiting in particular, one of their projects.

I am not unmindful of the warning about friendly visiting given me by a wise and experienced parish priest with whom I discussed its need. His feeling may be shared by other priests who are so often in and out of homes on pastoral visits and sick calls, and who are so sensitive to the attitudes of those they visit.

"You just can't keep popping in on the neighbors," he told me. "They won't like it, especially when they're old or sick. The house is apt to be untidy—clothes in disorder, dishes in the sink, dust all over—particularly if they live alone. They're ashamed to have you see it, and they're always afraid you'll go away and talk about how they live. They think everybody will gossip about them, and they'll never live it down."

Conditions such as he described are common and understandable. It is understandable, too, why these people so in need of visiting are not ashamed to have a priest or a doctor or a nurse see how they live. They need their services too much, and besides they know that priests and doctors and nurses are professional people who have seen many homes in the same condition and who, above all, do not gossip about what they see. But they think of friendly visiting as purely social occasions for which, all their lives, they have been accustomed to put their "best foot forward." And, more important, they know from experience that neighbors talk.

Yet Father's objection is not, essentially, as much to the visiting as it is to the visitor. Given a visitor impelled by the right motives, who is genuinely friendly and wants to help, and can be trusted not to talk about her visit except to pass on word of the needs she finds to those who can supply them—such a visitor, I know, would receive the pastor's blessing, and he would be the first to supply her with names and addresses.

No special training is needed to do the friendly visiting that is so important to old people, but certain qualities are necessary. First, I would put love of neighbor, growing out of love for God. The fact that we are not conscious of loving the neighbors we visit need not hold us back, if we remember God's "as if" formula: act *as if* we love them and we will come to love them. Friendly visiting in itself puts the formula to work.

We must feel that it is a matter of conscience that we do not talk about our visits except when necessary and to the proper people. Certainly we must never gossip outside the homes of those we visit, nor inside either. If, from habit or from a desire to brighten the conversation, we gossip about other people, the one we visit cannot be blamed for feeling that we will gossip about her as soon as we get out of the house.

It is not hard to make conversation that is not gossip, or to make our conversation interesting if we direct it to the person we are visiting and do not keep talking about ourselves. Interesting things going on in the neighborhood or at church will fill a pleasant half hour. There should be no recital, of course, of our own ills or of "Uncle Joe whose case was just like yours, may he rest in peace." And we should not talk too much because old people tire easily.

Actually we will not have to do much talking in most cases because old and sick people like to talk about themselves and our greatest service will be as listeners. Interested listeners are a rare treat to most of them. We will not find it difficult to be interested in the hundredth recital of events that happened long ago, if we will remember the joy it gives them to relive the past. If their recital should be, instead, an account of their ailments and difficulties, we should be understanding but not overly sympathetic. Pouring on the sympathy will not help but only make them more sorry for themselves.

It is better to visit frequently for short periods than less frequently for longer ones. An hour a week on schedule is better than longer visits "when we find time."

Our visiting hour should include something besides conversation. There will usually be little jobs we can do, especially if the person we visit lives alone. Perhaps we can wash a few dishes, or make a cup of tea, or tidy the place. Unless there is an emergency, however, and we have come in specifically to do bigger jobs like cooking and cleaning and laundry, we should do just a few of the small ones we can see need doing, and we should do them quickly and without apparent effort. A big job would appear to take us out of the "friendly visitor" class and make of us busybodies who "just had to get down and scrub that floor—my dear, you never saw anything so dirty!"

There is good reason for taking on a small job or two when we visit. It proves our desire to be helpful, and it brings us a little closer to those we visit because we give something of ourselves as well as of our time. When a visitor does nothing but sit and talk, there is bound to be a little strain. But when talk follows household activity, however small, a more intimate relationship develops because the visitor is no longer an outsider. She has shared in the work of the home.

If the person we visit does not live alone, we must confine the kind of work we do to little personal services: plumping up the pillows, straightening the spread, arranging a few flowers we have brought from our garden, offering to show her a "new" method of feeling good by giving her hair a good brushing. Household activities in this case might seem to reflect upon the others in the family and be resented, as if we felt they were not doing all they should, unless of course we see that they are overburdened and might appreciate our offer to help.

Most old people, and sick people, like us to read to them. Short selections are best, because their attention span is short as a child's. I find the *Catholic Digest* and *Reader's Digest* helpful, because all the selections are short, and the subjects are so varied that among them there are sure to be some that will be of interest. A woman I know who does a good deal of friendly visiting in her neighborhood tells me that many of the old people she visits, both Catholics and non-Catholics, like her to read a chapter from the Bible at each visit.

It is better not to make the first visit unannounced, or as Father expressed it "pop in" unexpectedly, especially if we do not know the people very well. If they have a telephone, it is thoughtful to call the day before, and give some reason for the visit: "May I stop in tomorrow afternoon and bring you some of our roses—they're beautiful this year"; or "Some of the women were asking about you, and I promised to stop in and see how you are. Is tomorrow afternoon a good time?" Such advance warning gives them time to straighten up a bit, and to look forward to our visit.

When we leave, we should tell them the day and time we will be back for another visit, and let nothing short of a catastrophe keep us from being there. Many old people live from visit to visit and count the hours between.

I seem to keep referring to the visitors and those visited as being strictly female, but of course this is not so. Many old men are greatly in need of friendly visiting, and men make their best visitors. Elderly widowers who have never had to look after themselves, nor even pick up their clothes, are most in need of neighborly help. If the old man lives alone, a male visitor can plunge in and do what needs doing—cleaning up, washing dishes, or doing what repair jobs he can. Even if the man lives with his family, little repair jobs are always appreciated. A male visitor might arrive with a few handgrips and offer to put them up in convenient spots to make it easier for the old man to get around.

Friendly visiting, whether on our own or as members of a parish society, helps us as much as it helps those we visit, as long as it is a personal apostolate and not a committee-and-casework affair. Because while reading to Mrs. Jones, or driving Mrs. Brown to Mass, or listening to Grandpa Green reminisce, we discover that they are not "cases" at all, but people. A committee cannot love, nor can a "case" be loved. It takes people to love and be loved, and it is in people that our love of Christ grows.

Christ commanded us to love our neighbors as ourselves. When He sends us next door to one of them, whether that neighbor is a Catholic, a Jew, a Protestant, or an atheist, we can be sure of the one thing necessary: He will be waiting there for us.

XIII

Blind Spot

I WENT to a senior prom not long ago. I didn't really belong because I wasn't one of the seniors. But I had a wonderful time, just being a wallflower, and watching.

Most of all I watched Mary and John. I do not know what their real names were, but those will do. Mary was dressed in a pretty pink print and had a flower in her hair. John wore a well-brushed blue suit. Whenever the music struck up, Mary would make her way over to John and take his hand, and John would tuck her hand under his arm and lead her out on the dance floor. To watch them dance, John so gallant and Mary so happy, was enough to break your heart.

Because Mary was seventy-six. And John was eighty-one and blind. And, more than that, John had a leg that was little use to him without a stout cane. But Mary's arm must have made a fine substitute, or perhaps the long-forgotten tunes had a limbering magic to them, because John would leave the cane on his chair whenever Mary came for him. They would dance, and all you could see was a tall lad in his best blue suit and a pretty girl with a flower in her hair.

Oh, it was a fine party, this "senior prom." I have been to teen-age parties and college-age parties and married-folks' parties, but I've never been to a party where people had as much fun as did these old folks, the senior members of the Church of St. Paul the Apostle, the Paulist Fathers' church in New York City.

The youngest senior there was a stripling of sixty-five. The oldest was a gentle little lady who would admit only that she had passed ninety quite a while back. There were a couple of hundred of them making merry in the parish hall.

It was a grand evening. There was the man who sang songs, with everybody joining in the choruses. There was the well-known actress (herself an aging woman), who told long-ago stories. There was the trip to the "art exhibit," where little ceramic figurines—proud results of the group's afternoon sessions—stood resplendent on shelves. And always there was the infectious accordion that brought everybody out to fill the dance floor between "numbers."

There were lots of attractions, but it was easy to see that one of the greatest was their beloved pastor. He was every place at once, greeting people by first names, inquiring about special problems and states of health (when you get on in years, the best medicine in the world is just being remembered), seeking out the solitary seniors and surrounding them with happy groups.

Toward the end of the evening when Father called out: *"Come and get it!"* the seniors trooped into the next room to chatter for half an hour around long tables while the "juniors" of the parish served them coffee and cake. Father was at the door as they left, with a handclasp and a bit of joshing that would keep each warm, until next time, with the feeling of being wanted.

"It takes so little," he said as he watched them go, "to make them happy. And it means so much. We knock ourselves out for youth today and forget the old people who gave us our youth and built our churches."

I thought of the young priests I have known, gray before their time trying to figure out ways of attracting young people to parish activities. I thought of the pastors worrying over the dwindling attendance at parish society meetings. And then I thought of these old folks to whom a few hours in the parish hall was the big, breath-taking, brimming-over event that lighted and warmed each week; who were so eager, so everlastingly grateful just to get together, to be remembered.   .

As a comparison of efforts and attitudes, it was too obvious to be missed. But as premises designed to lead up to some sort of conclusion, my train of thought was illogical. Because they are separate problems, and a parish cannot decide to give up its youth work as a thankless job, or abandon its marrieds to TV, just because the old folks are so responsive to a bare minimum of effort and expense.

Parishes know the importance of youth work, for our young people are the future of our Church and our country. We see only too clearly the problem of the booming birth rate in the bursting seams of our schools and our pitiful shortage of teachers. On every level, parochial, diocesan and national, the Church is working with and for youth.

Parishes know, too, the importance of active, alert, adult Catholics, of an informed and zealous laity, the present of the Church and a healthy and vigorous fifth of the American community. Through Catholic Action, the lay apostolate, the press, Cana conferences, retreats, study clubs, societies, the Church is constantly seeking to integrate every area of adult activity into fruitful Christian living.

But parishes have a blind spot, and it is growing more dangerous daily. They have forgotten the old folks. They look upon the old folks as "the past," to be respected, inquired after, looked in upon by the St. Vincent de Paul men, given the last rites when the time comes.

What parishes forget is that the old folks are no longer "the past." They are an ever-growing present. They are mushrooming into the major problem of the future of every parish, as of every community, in America. Parishes have a huge economic stake in their welfare. The problem is like a roof that can be kept in repair with little effort, but that can come crashing down about our heads if neglected too long.

Geriatrics is discovering much about the physical care of the old. The government, business and industry are attempting to provide at least for the subsistence needs of the aged. But man lives not by bread alone, nor by cortisone nor ACTH nor by any miracle of medical science. The whole man, body and soul, must be cared for—and this is where the parishes come in. It is the easiest, the least expensive, the most important and the most neglected job of all. The parish job is keeping the old people *happy*.

It is so simple a job that it seems ridiculously inadequate as any sort of solution to the staggering problem longevity is becoming. But its results are out of all proportion to the effort required. Keeping the old people happy, letting them know that they are both remembered and wanted, may not cure the physical evil of a lame leg or a deafened ear, but it does cure the attendant spiritual evils.

Friendly visiting is part of the parish job. Establishing day care and recreation centers for the aged is another. These centers may be called "Golden Age Clubs" or "Senior Citizens' Clubs" or "Hi Neighbor Clubs," but by any name they bring the old people out of their rooms, off the shelf and into happy companionship and activities with their contemporaries.

Every block of every parish today has its quota of old folks. Some live with children, some alone in bleak furnished rooms. Some live in reasonable comfort, some in squalor.

Some are fiercely independent, working at what jobs they can get. Some just wait out their lonely days.

Friendly visitors can seek out those who are able to attend day centers and encourage them to do so, perhaps accompanying them to the first meeting so they will not feel strange, or arranging regularly to drive a group of them who may need transportation.

But actually parishes need not seek them out. The old folks seek out the parishes that offer them companions and a place to meet these companions. When the program started at St. Paul's, a simple announcement brought fifty old people to the first get-together. Word spread over the grapevine so swiftly that within three months more than two hundred were turning out.

This group meets once a week for an afternoon of talk, games and hobby work. About once a month they have an evening social with music, dancing, simple refreshments and "entertainment," activities at which they are alternately spectators and participants so the evening will not prove too tiring. Willing entertainers can usually be found in the parish, and it is heart-warming to see how gladly "name" entertainers volunteer to come when they hear what is going on. But the best talent is the kind that can be found among the old people themselves, however hesitant or stumbling.

So great is the need for these centers that they should not be the responsibility solely of our Catholic and Protestant parishes and our Jewish congregations. Every neighborhood should have its own, finding a meeting place in the area that is easily accessible to those who cannot travel far. Public schools might open their doors during after-school hours once or twice a week for a community-sponsored center for the aged.

Little is needed for this vital work: a room to meet in, chairs enough for all, facilities for games and hobby work and a "master of ceremonies." This last might be the pastor or one of his assistants, or a man (not too young) of the neighborhood who has a happy personality and a knack of getting along with people. The old people need direction and encouragement. They are shy at first, so closely are they wrapped in the feeling of not being wanted. Hobby work, however simple, seems beyond them if it is unfamiliar, but what pride they take in their handiwork once they have been cajoled into trying! The "master of ceremonies" keeps things going, keeps things happy, keeps an eye on every individual to make sure none is ever left on the shelf.

Day-care centers or clubs can be important facilities of homes for the aged. There is a lively one affiliated with the home where I visited Mr. and Mrs. Hancock. Open to men, women and couples living in the area who are close to sixty years of age and over, its purpose is to bring companionship, contentment, and the enjoyment of stimulating activities and creative work into the lives of these aging people, and to extend the facilities of the home to those who are unable or not ready to enter it.

"Every home for the aged has its waiting list," the Mother Superior of the home says, "and some of these can join the club. Others do not need to go to a home for the aged, but suffer greatly from loneliness and need the companionship of others. Our facilities are open to them daily."

With the club open from eleven to five each day, and again from seven to nine each evening, members participate in such activities as choral groups, dancing, music appreciation, arts and crafts, dramatics, movies, games and cards. The old people are not only entertained, but form entertainment activities of their own. An interesting aspect of this center is that members have available to them the extensive facilities under which the geriatric program of the home functions, involving practically all departments of medical care for elderly people except major surgery.

Ordinarily, day-care centers for old people conducted by parishes, civic and neighborhood groups must confine themselves to simple recreational facilities. The importance and need of such work, simple and inexpensive though it is, cannot be overemphasized. But, as the need grows, a trend is becoming apparent to extend facilities into other areas of the old folks' lives, in order to make care more complete and more helpful.

An outstanding example of this trend is seen in the work being done by a center sponsored by Cardinal Mooney in Detroit. Its spirit is indicated by the words of Robert Browning which are inscribed over its entrance: "The best is yet to be, the last of life for which the first was made." Dedicated to the welfare of the growing numbers of aging men and women uprooted from familiar environments and forced to live on inadequate retirement incomes, the Detroit center is both a day club for any old person who wishes to walk in, and headquarters for a smaller group which enjoys its unique "on campus" plan of living.

Blaming compulsory retirement and unrealistic retirement plans that bear no relation to the cost of living for most of the old people's problems, the priest-director of the center says: "It is like putting two and two together and getting four. If industry and labor insist upon retiring able-bodied men and women at sixty-five while the doctors teach them to live until eighty or ninety, you have got to do something about all the years in between.

"I never saw such things until I got into this work," he adds. "You have no idea of the dirt and misery, the rotten food and utter neglect of elementary health measures that I found among retired people trying to live by themselves.

They wanted to be independent, they dreaded the restraints of an institution, they had no wish to impose themselves upon their children even if they might, but they did not know how to manage. You will hardly believe this, but the thing they need most is counsel. They have a little money, but they are bewildered in a changed status. They do not know which way to turn. They seldom know their rights."

The Detroit center's unusual "on campus" plan is a significant step ahead in the facilities of day-care centers, a pattern that may well be followed by other centers. Under it, the center finds clean, warm rooms in the neighborhood for its members and feeds them three good meals a day, in addition to giving them, as it gives the old people who avail themselves only of its day-care facilities, companionship, recreation, a chance to exercise their talents or skills, medical care and spiritual guidance.

The "on campus" plan at present is suffering from too much success. All available rooms within easy walking distance of the center have been filled with members, and the center is now planning to expand into a wider area by using buses to transport people from rooms found for them all over the city.

Feeding its "on campus" members three substantial meals a day runs into many thousands of meals each month, and involves a staggering amount of food and of cooking. Its success depends, as any successful effort to aid the aging must depend, upon community cooperation. Aside from a full-time chef and an occupational therapist to supervise the classes, all work is done by volunteers—individuals, clubs and societies.

The center pays out about ninety dollars a month for each "on campus" member, which includes about twenty-five dollars for a room and sixty-five dollars for meals.

"If they can afford that much, fine," says the director. "If they cannot—well, that's why we're here."

One old woman, for example, has no income except her monthly Social Security check for fifty-six dollars. Each month she endorses this over to the center in full payment for her room and board. And from it, in evidence of the depth of understanding that helps make its operation so successful, the center returns six dollars to her for "spending money."

Another old woman enjoying the facilities of the center summed up her feelings about it by speaking of the aspect that most impressed her.

"Everybody here has plenty to do," she said. "The institution where I lived before coming here was lovely, but all we did was eat turnips and look out the windows."

"On campus" members are watched as carefully by the center as a mother hen watches her chicks. Attendance at meals is checked, for if a member misses even one meal, illness is suspected. A doctor or a nurse may be needed, and meals in bed may have to be provided. In addition, the rooms occupied by these members must be checked on constantly to make sure they are kept clean and up to the center's standards. Continuous contact is maintained with city and social agencies.

The Detroit center, started in 1954, took over a big armory-like hall for its operations and converted it into club and classrooms, clinic, exhibition room, gift shop, dining room and stage. Community cooperation has been evident in all phases of its operation. A doctor and nurse come every week from the Detroit Board of Health. Many of its Catholic members attend daily Mass at the church next door, and a priest comes to conduct a day of meditation each month. Local attorneys offer legal advice, and give generously of their time because there is a continuous demand for counsel. Each month, one of Detroit's prominent clubs sends over a supply of bus tickets for day members who live too far away from the center to walk to classes easily. When the center put on its arts and crafts show last year, to exhibit and sell the old folks' handiwork, Detroit's newspapers cooperated by devoting so much space to publicizing it that the hall was packed with people eager both to see and to buy. This year the show is to be sponsored in cooperation with Detroit's Historical Museum, and held in the museum's fine exhibition room.

A day-care center, like a seed, can be planted within a single neighborhood block, and grow from such small beginnings into organizations with the scope and tremendous accomplishments of the Detroit center. If we are able to start on a larger scale, to get the ear of civic leaders and their cooperation with facilities and space in which to conduct the center, we are better off because we are able to start with a seedling instead of a seed and growth will be faster. But no more is really necessary than neighborly concern. Nothing can grow until it has been started in however small a way. As Mother Cabrini once said: "Action is the thing. *Get it started*. Then, if it is God's will, it will continue and prosper."

Any one of us, as individuals, can start by getting together with the neighbors on the block, and talking over the need of doing something for our old people. Quarters might be found in a neighbor's playroom, or we can all pitch in to clean and decorate a neighbor's roomy basement, lend chairs, tables, phonograph and records, and perhaps a vintage piano. A very few dollars will provide sufficient hobby materials and inexpensive cups and saucers, and willing hands will be found to build shelves on which to display the results of the old people's handiwork.

Old people on the block and in surrounding blocks can be invited in one afternoon or evening a week, or oftener, at regular hours convenient to the neighbor donating the space and to the "master of ceremonies" who volunteers to direct activities and keep things happy. Refreshments should be of the simplest, prepared and served by two or three of the women. Even more can be accomplished by delegating the responsibility of refreshments and the cleaning of the room to the teen-agers on the block. Introducing them early to such service will shape both their future and ours beyond belief. "Dues" of fifty cents or a dollar a month from each neighbor on the block is enough, at the beginning, for the food served and for hobby materials.

This is an apostolate cut to our measure that will multiply like the loaves and the fishes Our Lord distributed, and for the same reason: God will be working with us.

Providing for the needs of the aged among us is one of the best and most effective ways of preparing for our own later years. Starting and supporting day-care and recreation centers on parish, community and block levels, like initiating parish programs of friendly visiting, is insurance that when our time comes we shall not lack activities to fill those years, counsel and care to lighten them, and companions to warm them like a fire on the hearth. It will be good to remember that we were the ones who supplied the kindling and struck the first spark.

XIV

"The Truest Story"

A FEW MONTHS AGO I received an invitation to attend the thirtieth reunion of my college class. It made me feel ancient, although I am sure I can never feel quite as old and wise as I did on that June morning long ago when I adjusted the tassel on my mortarboard and marched solemnly up to receive the sheepskin that testified (in Latin, as if meant for the understanding and acknowledgment of generations) that I was a Bachelor of Arts, having absorbed the required measure of education. What I was to do with it was not specified, but I had no doubt that whatever I did would play a recognizable part in changing the world's course for the better.

But I quickly lost my "bachelor" status, and the arts that I had acquired became dusty as I grew busy learning others: the art of diaper-changing, of whipping up meals that by some magic would feature everybody's favorite every day, of budgeting a household where the unexpected is the usual. Those earlier arts had not been wasted, however. It was not long before I had to dust them off and use them to help me stimulate growing minds and shape growing personalities and guide growing interests into promising channels.

"Come to Reunion!" urged the invitation. "Tell us all about yourself and your doings on the enclosed questionnaire!"

The questionnaire was a lengthy one, and when I had answered mine it was not very interesting even to me. This month, when reunion time arrived, all the answers to all the questionnaires had been compiled and analyzed by patient former classmates who apparently are not driven mad by that kind of work.

I found that three-quarters of us are married and practically none of us divorced. But our birth rate is almost as negligible as our divorce rate. Only half of us have children and those among us who are proud parents have produced, statistically, only 1.95 children each. Most of us have been busy about many things, earning graduate degrees, teaching, writing, running things.

I do not doubt that some of us are making worth-while contributions to society, though we are hardly helping to perpetuate it, but somehow I felt terribly let down when I read the published results. It reminded me of the "busy work" my children have in school every once in a while. When the teacher wants to catch up on her records and reports, she gives them anything that comes to mind just to keep them busy.

So much fuss and furore over so very little! I searched the results for something more interesting, and found it under hobbies.

"Here's where we show ourselves up," the report states. "Your life's work may be happenstance but the job you do for fun or love tells the truest story of you."

We have two and three-quarters hobbies apiece which are more, it might be noted, than we have children. Reading and gardening are the most popular, with music and travel next. About a third admit to traditionally housewifely hobbies—cooking, needlework and the like—and an equal number to sports.

Among our other hobbies that, if we are to believe the report, tell "the truest story" of ourselves, are listed flower arranging, collecting pennies, playing cards and bird watching—not to overlook one woman who listed, as her favorite outdoor sport, "neighbor watching." Two honest souls said their hobby was "being lazy in the sun." And of all of us who so solemnly accepted, that bright June morning, the responsibility of the measure of education we had received, only six of us listed church, club or community work as hobbies.

To be fair to my classmates, I suppose that many of us (even the neighbor watcher and the two lazy sun bathers) are doing worth-while work in our homes or businesses or professions, and a few of us, I am sure, have done rather important things. I cannot help wondering, however, how many of us realize the importance of hobbies.

Webster defines a hobby as "any favorite pursuit, topic or object; that which a person persistently pursues with zeal or delight."

The work at which we earn our living may be a favorite pursuit and we may perform it with zeal and great delight. If so, we have been blessed beyond measure. But, unless it is our own business or profession, it will slip from our grasp some day when we reach a compulsory retirement age, or perhaps vanish with a change of management or the whim of an employer.

Even if the work we love is our own, the time may come when we are unable to continue it; it may exceed the physical strength of our later years, or require a fine degree of coordination or acute eyesight that we no longer possess. The kind of work at which we are successful during our active productive years is not, ordinarily, the kind that can be continued without lessening of output and income when God begins to slow us down.

Hobbies are activities apart from the work that supports us. They are the little lifeboats strung along the sides of our ship. They do not look like very much in comparison, but they are going to look mighty good to us when the ship founders, or when our own engine trouble slows it to a stop. We will still have a long way to go home, and we will have to use a lifeboat. It will be tragic if we find that our lifeboats, so decorative and amusing strung alongside through the years, are not seaworthy to support us when we need them.

Hobbies stay with us through life, though their importance is not evident—except as needed relaxation or change of pace—during our active years. Yet, actually, these years are an apprenticeship during which we develop the interests and skills which will be important to us later on. Our years of active work are the years given us to build resources for our later years, with hobbies that can help others, enrich ourselves and support us if need be.

Those of us who have no hobbies should start developing some now. All hobbies require a little time and work, if they are to be worth-while. If we feel we haven't the time, we must realize the importance of making time. And as for the work needed to develop skill in our chosen hobbies, we are equal to such work now, but may not be up to mastering new skills later on when we find ourselves being cut down to size.

It is not hard to find a hobby that we can "pursue with zeal or delight." The improvement of some special skill or the widening of some special area of knowledge is always a challenge and, if pursued with zeal, always a delight.

How to choose a hobby? It is not enough to decide to start collecting early American glass just because our friend

Mrs. Adams does, or to start a home workshop just because a retired neighbor down the street gets so much enjoyment from his, unless of course these pursuits awaken a lively interest in us and keep intruding on our workaday thoughts and nudging us to get started.

It often happens that we find some small part or aspect of our daily work so interesting that we keep wishing we had more time to devote to it on our own. If so, we have an excellent start toward a worth-while hobby, and will be able to expand it with the skill and knowledge we have acquired through the years. If not, we can look back upon some of the things that interested us before our busy years absorbed us. The things that interested us in our youth, and which we may have had to drop because of pressures upon us, will usually be found just as interesting when we take them up again. They are easy to revive, and fit naturally into our inclinations. Or there may be certain activities we have run across during our active years that appealed to us strongly, but that we had to dismiss for lack of time.

If we already have hobbies it is wise to evaluate them with an eye to the future, just as we should apply a critical yardstick to new hobbies we are considering.

First, how much will we be able to do in our later years? None of us knows the limitations which may be imposed upon us as the years mount, and how much strength, sight, coordination or concentration we may be capable of. But certain hobbies, however enjoyable now, are obviously unsuitable for lifetime enjoyment.

We may thrill to the challenge and exhilaration of mountain climbing now, but even the gentle slope to the base of our favorite mountain is apt to be too great an exertion for us in five, ten or twenty years. I knew a retired Protestant minister who was devoted to mountain climbing all his life. We called him "The Little Minister." He was little, lean

and lithe, and he kept his climbing boots handy. He cele-
brated his seventieth birthday by scaling a new peak—new,
that is, to him. But he was always saddened by the fact that
not one of his contemporaries, all enthusiastic members of
his climbing club, had been able to accompany him for
years. He was definitely an exception and, of course, there
is always the possibility that he would have lived longer if
he had respected his natural limitations a little more.

When we have chosen a hobby or hobbies which we can
reasonably expect to continue and enjoy during our later
years, we should apply another kind of yardstick to them:
Are they the kind that will enable us, in some way, to help
others? Are they the kind that will help enrich ourselves by
keeping us alert and interested, giving us a sense of achievement, satisfying us and making of us more satisfying people
to know and to be with? Are they the kind that can, if
necessary, earn us an after-retirement income?

There are many single hobbies that can do all three. If
ours does not we need not abandon it, but simply add a
hobby or two to fill these very real requirements.

Painting has expanded into one of our most popular
hobbies during recent years, aided perhaps by Grandma
Moses' success, and by the love of painting for creative
relaxation enjoyed by such busy people as President Eisen-
hower and Winston Churchill. A blank piece of canvas offers exciting invitation, and one's first painting, however
crude, gives a heady sense of achievement. There are classes
we can attend, but we do not really need training to enjoy
the fun of painting. My brother, who is in his early forties,
took up portrait painting (admittedly the most difficult kind)
as a hobby because faces fascinated him. He taught himself
by doing. Now, ten years later, he has as many commissions
as he can handle during his free hours, and has an exhibition
of his paintings each year. Only in exceptional cases, how-

ever, will painting earn us a livelihood when our regular workaday income stops.

Painting can, however, be turned into a supplementary income if need be. We can hold classes for other amateurs, especially for our contemporaries, and introduce them to the creative joy of brush and canvas. We will find a ready market for small paintings of neighbors' homes or of their favorite scenic spots. It will take more skill to paint their children or their pets, but with practice we may be able to achieve good likenesses.

Ceramics is another fascinating hobby. A kiln of our own, or the use of another's, is needed for it. One woman I know has a good market for a combination of two hobbies, painting and ceramics. She paints tiles, illustrating them with scenes ordered by her customers, or with anniversary, birthday or Christmas designs and personally inscribed greetings that her customers wish to give as gifts.

Reading is a never-ending source of enjoyment and enrichment. It is a little shocking how seldom many of us, even those of us with college educations and graduate degrees, read worth-while books regularly. We may think we do, but if we should jot down the name of each book as we finish it, we would be apt to find a very skimpy list at the end of a year's time. Most of us read newspapers and magazine articles on the run, and feel that our limited time justifies our being satisfied with condensations of popular books so that we may at least be able to hold our own in conversations about them.

We hear much about developing reading rapidity these days and some remarkable things are being done to speed our reading-words-per-minute. Special reading-training classes, such as those given at New York University's Reading Institute, are being offered in the adult-education programs of many schools. For those of us aware of the importance of reading, and who are truly limited in the time we can devote to it, speeding our rate may be the answer to getting more reading done. It must be emphasized, however, that a faster rate does not mean skipping or scanning, or breezing through light fiction or the latest whodunit, but rather reading unfamiliar material of moderate difficulty with full comprehension and retention.

The average college graduate has a reading speed of 225 to 250 words a minute in textbook or source material and manages, with the help of special reading classes, to double his speed to 450 to 500 words a minute.

Would you like to test yourself? It might be enlightening.

Have someone time you on a moderately difficult text that is unfamiliar to you. Mark off how much you read in sixty seconds, then hand the book to your questioner. Don't try merely to repeat parts of it; a "play-back" tests only memory, and not comprehension. Instead, try to summarize in one or two sentences what the author has said. Then try to give the meaning of the whole passage and see if you can answer inference questions on it.

I must point out that my mother, who finds in reading one of the greatest enjoyments of her later years and who reads more books in a month than I do in a year, scoffs at the whole idea of programs to speed our reading rate.

"What on earth do people want to read *fast* for?" she asks. "That would take away all my pleasure in it. I enjoy reading slowly so I can savor every word."

That's the way I read, too. But if I trained myself to read faster, with comprehension and retention, I might find equal pleasure in it and certainly I would be able to do a lot more reading. It is something to consider during these years when our time is limited, in order to establish a rewarding hobby for our more leisurely years.

Music is a similarly rewarding hobby, whether we take it

up as performers or listeners. Most of us "took piano" when we were young, or perhaps scraped away on a pint-sized violin, and then dropped it as school and work demanded so much of our time. It is surprising how much of it comes back to us, and how much more enjoyable it is to work on even the simplest pieces from the vantage point of the years.

Many old people, who have never played an instrument before, take music lessons with pleasure and profit. They do not expect to become accomplished musicians, but they develop a never-ending source of enjoyment for themselves and (sometimes) for their families and friends. In recent years the recorder has come back into its own. It is a true musical instrument, yet it is easy to learn, simple to play, and can afford endless pleasure to individuals and to groups. If you have ever heard a trio or a quartet of old people playing together, however inexpertly, you may not thrill to the sounds they produce, but you will never forget their rapt expressions.

To be able to listen to music properly, even if we do not participate actively, can also be richly rewarding. It takes a little time and study during our active years when we are able to get to recitals and concerts, but it is supremely worth-while. Much good music may be heard on the radio and occasionally on television. Accumulating a collection of fine recordings for home enjoyment adds to our interest and builds a "stockpile" to enrich the less active years ahead.

My mother is an accomplished musician, but the violin with which she used to delight great audiences has been stilled for many years. Stiffening fingers have turned her from performer to listener but have not diminished her enjoyment of music. She spends several hours each day listening to recordings, and when guests are present she selects records to provide a well-rounded concert.

"The different voices speak to me," she says of the instruments that blend into a symphony. "It's like listening to an exciting conversation. Each voice has something different to say about the theme; sometimes something important, and sometimes an amusing little aside. Sometimes there are arguments, and you hear the different opinions being resolved. There's always a happy ending in classic works. In some modern works, they keep arguing right to the end. I never tire of listening."

If you have a "green thumb," gardening can be one of the most satisfying of hobbies. There is something thrilling and almost holy about watching things grow. It is a kind of sharing in God's creation. Preparing the soil, planting, cultivating, watching flowers grow to glory or vegetables to the harvest is only part of the enormous pleasure gardeners know. There is equal enjoyment in planning a garden. And experimentation can provide an exciting hobby: selecting and cross-breeding strains to produce a new type or size or coloring of flower or vegetable.

Specializing also adds interest. I know a woman who has a "Mary Garden" which includes every variety of blue flower. Her garden is in bloom from spring till fall, a little patch of earth that reflects the blue sky above it and rejoices the hearts of all who see it. I have heard of a garden filled with "Biblical" plants, all the flowers and vegetables and herbs that are mentioned in the Bible. I know of a man who grows flowers especially for the altar of his parish church and to distribute to nearby hospitals. He is repaid for his work, many times over, in the joy he gives to others. Even those who have limited space, who live in apartments or furnished rooms, can do wonders with window boxes. Whole herb gardens can be grown, and their products used to season our food or to sell to the neighbors. A family I know of has a mushroom farm in the basement. Mushrooms, which are easy and quick to grow, provide a continuing and profitable harvest.

Fish and animals also make absorbing hobbies and patience, and skill with them will repay any early failures. Tropical fish, in beautiful and almost infinite variety, need careful attention but no great physical exertion and can if we wish be built up into a profitable business. If we fancy raising dogs, cats or chickens, where we live and the space available will determine whether we can devote ourselves to such a hobby. But this kind of hobby takes time to learn, and a good deal of experience before we are ready to put it to income-producing use. Our joy at being allowed to feed the chickens long ago on Grandpa's farm is not sufficient training for raising them now. And a succession of pet dogs or cats in the house does not equip us to become breeders and raisers of them. If we love animals, now is the time to learn all we can about them and their care and raising. Or, if we do not want to go into it on a large scale, we will find such services as we are able to offer in good demand. People always want to find places to board pets when they plan a trip or vacation; if we can furnish them good care, clean quarters and a safe fenced-in yard, we should be well supplied with paying guests.

We may decide to go in for a more specialized kind of animal hobby, such as raising turkeys, minks or chinchillas. There are many hazards involved in turkey raising, as in mink raising (especially the kind of mink that goes to market) and we must have the time and patience to become experts in the field before we attempt it.

A word of caution is necessary about raising chinchillas, a hobby that thousands of people through the country are eagerly undertaking, spurred on by the tremendous amount of publicity being given to it. A great deal of this publicity is misleading, especially that part of it that points to the tremendous profits to be realized.

Most of these eager amateur chinchilla breeders are in for heartbreak. Yes, good chinchilla skins are rare, and the very few garments made from them are extremely expensive. But the very rarity of the garments is what makes them so expensive. It takes only common sense, and an elementary knowledge of economics, to realize that as the thousands of chinchilla breeders flood the market with these skins, values and prices will plummet to earth. Therefore the effort would seem to be entirely on the part of those who sell the animals, and for their own profit. When the bubble bursts, a lot of hopes and investments are bound to break with it. The only way many hopefuls have been able to profit so far is to sell pairs of their animals to other hopefuls.

We must be wary of "get rich quick" schemes in planning our hobbies, unless we go into them for present enjoyment only, and without hope of future return. If we realize the promised return, well and good. But if we are going to need financial support, either total or partial, from hobbies in our later years, it is wiser to shun glowing promises.

Other people's promises are not so dependable as our own skill and effort. After all, it is our own future. And if we develop the skill and make the effort during our young and middle years, when skills come more easily and effort is stimulating instead of tiring, our future years can both satisfy and support us.

—•—

XV

Lifeboats

A NEIGHBOR OF MINE is a young teacher, struggling to support his family on an inadequate salary, and using most of his free time to work for his Master's degree which will increase his income somewhat. He and his wife have a baby and are expecting another, so that what time is left from school and studies he likes to spend helping in the house. But, though he is only in his twenties, he recognizes both the present and the future importance of a hobby, and manages to make time for it.

During his two years of army service, he went to photography school, where a top-quality professional course is condensed into sixteen weeks to turn out expert photographers. After this training, he spent the rest of his service time as an army photographer. Now he adds to his income by taking pictures of the children in the neighborhood, particularly the babies. Parents are eager to have pictures of their children, and spread word of his service so that he has an ever-growing list of clients. He is called in to take other pictures too, of birthday parties, anniversary celebrations and Christmas gatherings. His first album of pictures taken at a friend's wedding and reception brought him a good fee, and prospects for more such jobs.

"The extra money is certainly handy," he says. "I love

teaching even though I know that staying in the field will probably mean a struggle to make ends meet. But photography will always help out, and if I keep it up it will be good security when I retire."

Photography is a fascinating hobby whether or not we ever expect it to support us. An inexpensive camera and a few rolls of film are all we need to start. With these we will learn the rudiments and there are booklets to give us the basic rules of getting good pictures. But we should not be content with snapping pictures. Developing them is a major part of the enjoyment of this hobby. When we become more experienced we can experiment with special effects and finishes, and perhaps invest in an enlarger. When we ourselves do the whole job, from taking the picture to finishing the print or enlargement, we can take a creative joy in our work.

Creative work is the only kind of work that brings true satisfaction. Perhaps it is because we are human beings, made in the image of God, that our deepest instincts long to give Him glory by reflecting something of all His attributes and powers, even creation. Of course we can never actually create anything, for to create means to bring something forth from nothing. The best we can do is bring something forth from existing materials. But there is deep joy in seeing the results of applying our head and hands and heart to those materials.

Very often the reason why we find so little satisfaction in the work that earns our daily bread is that we do not feel it is creative. The industrial age has substituted the assembly line (and there are white-collar assembly lines too) for the old craftman's bench, and the hurry-up process to provide goods for the increasing demand has chopped our work up into little pieces, so that we lose all sense of the whole and thus lose joy in it. Many industries today realize this, and attempt to give their employees an over-all picture of the operation in order to inspire pride in the finished product or service, and to show each what an important contribution his own little part makes to the whole. The results, in improved management-employee relationships, morale, loyalty and output are astonishing, because the workers begin to feel a creative pride in what they do, understanding that their work is part of a whole creative effort.

As long as we are human, we will long to express ourselves in creative work and know the satisfying achievement of seeing work that is all ours, however imperfect. If our best efforts have gone into it, what we do will be as beautiful and satisfying to us and to those who love us as a child's first scribbled crayon drawing is to him and his parents. Since it is difficult for most of us to experience the joy of creation in our daily work, we must find it in a creative hobby.

Gardening, making music, raising animals and photography are only a few creative hobbies of the many that can be developed. Almost any of them will furnish lasting satisfactions to enrich our later years, as well as provide ways in which we can help others. Many of them can become income-producers if we start them working for us now so that they will provide us with support at the time we need it.

Cooking is a hobby, but usually not to the woman who must cook three meals a day. She may like to cook, and take a measure of creative joy in experimenting with new dishes or turning out a perfect cake. But our hobbies are something apart from our daily work. Thus businessmen may have cooking as a hobby, as an increasing number of them do. I know many men who are part-time chefs, taking vast pride in outdoor cooking, or monopolizing the kitchen to turn out a delectable steak or stir up their own "secret recipe" salad dressing. When the woman who cooks regularly also has cooking as her hobby, it is usually some specialty apart from the regular mealtime dishes she prepares: preserves, a good relish or special sauce, cookies or candy.

Needlework of all kinds (except darning and mending!) makes an excellent hobby. Knitting, crocheting, needlepoint, embroidering and weaving enable us to turn out useful and decorative objects for ourselves and others to enjoy, and will stand us in good stead in later years. Sewing can be an excellent income-producer if we develop our skill so that we can make garments that look professional and fit well. Many a woman supports herself after retirement by dressmaking, and those who do not need additional income are able to economize substantially by making their own clothes. Other women are skilled at alterations for which there is always a demand. Some women, who perhaps loved making doll clothes when they were young, specialize in making little girls' clothes, and some actually make doll clothes again!

One woman I know, who is approaching seventy, started dressing dolls a few years ago and distributing them at Christmas to the youngsters in a nearby hospital. It was difficult for her to buy the dolls out of her small income, but word soon spread, and now manufacturers donate the dolls, and the whole neighborhood donates scraps of material. It has grown into a neighborhood project, and many of the older women get together throughout the year to dress the dolls in bright silks and cottons, velvet and lace, to make wan little faces light up with the splendor of Christmas.

Another woman specializes in fine baby clothes. During her years in business, she had taken time to make a beautiful little dress and matching slip for each new baby in the family. Before she retired, orders had been coming in from friends who wanted them for their babies, or to give as treasured gifts. When she lost what money she had, through a series of misfortunes after retirement, her friends gathered together a few of the dresses she had made and showed them to the infant-wear buyers at several smart shops. There were immediate orders. She has as much work as she can handle today, and enjoys a comfortable income. Fortunately, her eyes are still sharp and her fingers still skillful enough for the tiny stitches and minute tucks she lavishes upon the little garments.

Knitted garments have a ready market. So do hand-hooked rugs, although these are harder to handle and heavier to work, and may some day be beyond our strength unless we organize a group and share the work.

There are few men who do not like to work with their hands, and many of them love to saw and plane wood, build it into something, rub it to a loving finish, and produce it proudly that others may admire. There is a satisfaction in carpentry and woodworking that few other hobbies can provide. The job at hand may be no more than repairing the porch steps, or putting up some extra shelves in the kitchen. But once the good feel of wood and smell of sawdust have been experienced, there is no stopping a man. He will want to go on furnishing his house with things he himself makes, and know the joy of early craftsmen who had to do just that. A skilled carpenter or cabinet maker, or simply a skilled repairman, will never lack an income.

All of the sciences await us, ready to brighten our later years with the exhilaration of expanding knowledge. We can become amateur astronomers and, as our knowledge grows, build a telescope of our own through which to scan the night skies. Meteorology is an absorbing subject; so is botany. The study of plants opens up a whole world of fascinating study in our own back yard and may lead to research and discoveries of our own. There are insects to study, a world of insect life as busy as our own, organized to peak efficiency, operating under its own laws, that can fill us with a saving humility. We can study minerals, rocks, leaves, shells and start our own collections of them.

Collecting is a favorite hobby and almost anything that is portable can be collected, unless of course it belongs to somebody else. You may be a "born" collector and not know it because you have not yet thought of collecting. If you like to arrange things and enjoy keeping them in order, chances are that collecting is for you. The "born" collector is not satisfied simply to accumulate a lot of things; those who "just can't bear to throw anything out" are not real collectors. Orderliness is as great a passion as acquisitiveness to a real collector, who takes as much pleasure in arranging and classifying the things he collects as he does in finding them.

You might start with something you already have and particularly like and go on from there. It might be a unique little pitcher, a piece of old silver, a few interesting old buttons or antique jewelry. Any one makes a good starting point for a collection. Of course stamps, coins and autographs are favorite collectors' items, as are glassware, prints, dolls, china, clocks and an almost endless list of others. I think I may be the only woman in the country who has a mother who collects camels. Yes, *camels*. Not live, of course, and not dead ones either—they're miniatures and look just as mean as their live counterparts. I once thought my unique distinction was being threatened when I met a woman who told me that *she* had a friend whose mother collects camels. But during the conversation she happened to mention her friend's name and the friend turned out to be my sister. Whatever you collect, be sure that you can continue to afford it. Unless you have plenty of money, don't decide to collect antique furniture, cars or prize paintings.

People are drawn together by hobbies into lasting friendships. Business acquaintances seldom become close friends,
because our daily work does not often reflect our deepest
interests. Friendships we make in the office or shop are
usually surface friendships, held together by the circumstance of having to be together for so many hours each
day within the same four walls. Friendships cannot be imposed from without, but must grow from within. When we
meet another who shares our interest in the same hobby
or the same study, there is an immediate bond. We will, in
fact, find clubs and organizations already established in
almost any field we choose for a hobby, and it is good to
seek them out because we will find that members share our
interest and enthusiasm, speak our language and are eager
to exchange information and offer us friendly and stimulating competition.

Many of us enjoy active sports and we should continue
them as long as we do not overdo. The aging tennis player
who comes puffing over the net to congratulate his younger
opponent is not the fine figure of a sportsman he imagines
himself. He is simply a foolish old man who will not be
able to answer the invitation of a freshly rolled court some
fine morning because his heart has given out. It is the
same with any strenuous activity. If we have been active in
a vigorous sport all our lives, and have kept ourselves in
condition, it may be possible to continue in a limited way if
the doctor checks up on us regularly. But in a sport, as in
everything else, it is wise to remember that moderation as
the years mount, far from diminishing our enjoyment, may
actually enable us to enjoy it for a longer period of time.

It is even wiser to cultivate one of the quieter sports
which we may reasonably expect to enjoy to the full through
all our years. Walking is the basis of most of them, and few
things are better for us than walking. When we walk in

search of a little ball, with a bag of clubs over our (or a caddy's) shoulder, we call it golf. If we walk with a gun under our arm, we call it hunting. Both can be as strenuous or as easy-going as we wish, and we should keep our limitations in mind. If we walk with a camera in hand we may return with rewarding shots of more lasting enjoyment than those we took with a gun. And if we walk with nothing but observant eyes, we will discover a wonderful new world.

Fishing is the philosopher's sport, in and out of season. Plans and dreams and tying flies can fill his off-season until spring sends him forth into the streams searching out new spots where the biting is good. Or he may do his fishing while dreaming the day away on a quiet bank, a sunny wharf or in a bobbing boat. Struggle with the great fish of the deep is no longer for him, but rather the pleasure of a small catch, or the equal pleasure of tossing it back in gratitude for a happy day.

Adult education is a hobby that has mushroomed over the past ten years to the point where courses are offered to everybody in almost anything. Of course if you wish to complete a high school or college education that was interrupted long ago, there is a required program of study leading to diploma or degree. Every June the newspapers carry pictures of happy grandmothers, and sometimes grandfathers, graduating along with son or daughter. They may want to put their diploma or degree to some specific use, but I imagine in most cases they worked for it because the unfinished business they left behind in the classroom kept nudging them and they wanted the satisfaction of completing it.

But if you are not working for diploma or degree, the field is wide open and you may choose courses in almost any subjects that interest you, running the roster from art, bridge and ceramics to xylophone, youth guidance and zoology. You might want to learn or brush up on a language, train your memory, try your hand at short-story writing or learn how to prepare income tax returns. This last will make you a popular person in your neighborhood when income tax time comes and you can do a good business in preparing returns for a fee.

The head of the Department of Adult Education at Brooklyn College, which is one of the largest such departments in the country, told me that they are willing to give a course in any subject under the sun, if at least ten students enroll for it. The same is true of many such schools. So if you can round up nine cronies who long to learn Sanskrit, or how to cook a crow so that it is palatable around election time, you will find a class and a teacher awaiting you.

Perhaps you are equipped to teach a course in an adult education program, either at a high school or college or at a center where many such programs are conducted as community enterprises. No college degree is necessary if your skill is a craft such as cooking, sewing, woodworking, painting, ceramics and the like. All that is required in most cases is a competency test. If you are fluent in a foreign language, you may be able to give conversation classes in it. It might be well to investigate the openings in your special hobby if experience has given you skill at it, or create an opening yourself by bringing along ten or more friends who would like to have you teach it to them. And, of course, there are many subjects or skills that you can teach privately to friends, either individually or in groups.

Whatever our hobby, if it is one we hope some day to turn into an income-producer (and we should have at least one such hobby as a "lifeboat") it is important to start it working for us now.

If it is a product we make, now is the time to iron out the kinks, to investigate the proper methods, packaging and distribution, to decide upon our market and the best ways of reaching it at lowest cost, to get the product launched if only in a small way. Needed improvement in the product itself, or in our methods of making and distributing it, will quickly show up. We may not be able to devote much time to it now, but at least we will have made a start. By the time we are ready to stop our active work, our hobby should be established and bringing us some sort of income. Our leisure time can then be devoted to promoting and expanding it, and need not be taken up with experimenting and launching it.

If it is a service we offer, the time to start offering it is now. When we are ready to lean on it for support, we shall have become known for it and our circle of clients will have grown far beyond our immediate acquaintances.

Community work can be the most rewarding hobby of all. I do not include parish work under the "hobby" heading, although it fits the definition as something we can and should pursue with zeal or delight, and it is apart from the work that earns our livelihood. Parish work is a more fundamental responsibility, just as our responsibilities to our families are not hobbies though they are distinct from our daily work.

Community work is also a responsibility, but it can be classified as a hobby because we can choose, from many kinds, the type of work and type of organization that interest us most, and because we can choose between community work and other hobbies, knowing that we are fulfilling our obligation to serve the community by working for our parish.

There is so much community work to be done, so many ways to do it, and all of them deeply satisfying. The Red Cross, the Community Chest, hospitals, orphanages and foundling homes, prisons, homes for the aged, institutions for the blind—the list is endless with a wide choice in almost every community. Volunteers are needed and eagerly sought and many organizations give them special training if needed.

Almost any skill we have can be put to worth-while use in the service of our community. We may be able to help by typing, filing, answering the telephone, working at the reception desk, rolling bandages, pushing library carts through the wards. If we drive a car, we may be able to chauffeur for one or more of these organizations, or take blind people out for occasional rides. The blind always welcome readers, too. In many communities free classes teach sighted people how to transcribe printed matter into Braille for the blind; volunteers who complete these courses do wonderful work transcribing everything from magazines to textbooks. Volunteers with love to spare are needed in orphanages and foundling homes to give the babies the cuddling that the overworked nurses have no time to give. And of course we can visit the hospitalized and run errands for them.

If our time and talents permit, we might help community causes by public speaking or helping in fund-raising and publicity programs. Something from everyone is needed; unskilled but willing workers are as welcome as experts in their fields.

Community work helps those who work at it, not only because they are part of the community being helped, but also in a more personal way. I saw its restorative power work wonders on a young business girl. After just one year of marriage, her husband died tragically. She was in a state of shock for some time, but as soon as it was possible for her to go back to the office she did, agreeing with her doctor and her family that a regular work routine would help her. But she lasted only two days and then went to pieces. Her understanding employers gave her an indefinite leave, and assured her of a welcome whenever she felt able to come back.

A few weeks later she walked in like a different girl. She was calm and poised and could even talk about her loss. She seemed to have grown up, in maturity and depth of perception, and told her friends that voluntary service to others in need had been her own life saver. After her breakdown at the office she had, almost in desperation, walked into a big veterans' hospital in the city and begged to be given any kind of job to do. She was assigned to run the moving picture machine in the paraplegic ward, and she spent her evenings doing it. It was mechanical work, the room was in merciful semi-darkness and she did not have to speak to any of the men, much less attempt to cheer them up. She found they did not need cheering up, at least while they watched the screen and she watched them. They scarcely knew she was there, changing reels and operating the machine behind them, but they renewed her courage and her hope, and sent her back to work her way once more to happiness through a useful, normal life.

There are many of us in our middle years who are finding the same sort of personal help in community work. This type of work, particularly in religious organizations, is a hobby that can fill our later years with contentment, useful service, and a sense of personal consecration.

Father Edward F. Garesche of the Catholic Medical Mission Board has seen many old people giving unselfishly of their energy and time, and knows at first hand the deep personal satisfaction and happiness this work gives them. He tells of one of them, a woman who had retired on a pension.

"When I gave up active work and began to live on my pension," she said to him, "I thought at first that I was going to have a grand time—no obligations, no work, no responsibilities. But I soon found time hanging on my hands. Sometimes I'd find myself just staring at the wall. Then I heard that the Catholic Medical Mission Board welcomed volunteers who could give a few hours a day to clerical work and other activities. So I volunteered—and what a difference it has made! Once more I have a useful occupation, I'm part of a vigorous active organization. But instead of helping make money for other people, I'm now helping to save souls, aid broken bodies and spread the light of Faith."

Community work is voluntary and so will not earn us an income. But it should be one of our hobbies because it is important both to the community and to us. We might choose it to fill the requirement that we have a hobby that helps others, and add another that will help support us when we need it.

We need not have too many lifeboats, but those we have should be kept in good repair and we should start now learning how to use them.

XVI

———•••———

Belonging

ONE OF THE BASIC NEEDS of every human being is to *belong*. The need to belong, and indeed the right to belong, was woven into the fibers of our being at birth, because we were created as social creatures. We might almost say that as individuals we were created incomplete, destined to find our completion in the society of our own kind.

Perhaps we do not often think of "belonging" as a basic need. That is because it is so basic that we don't think consciously of it any more than we think consciously of breathing. Yet if we should stop belonging, the results would be as drastic as if we should stop breathing.

"Oh, I'm not a 'joiner,'" some of us say, in turning down an invitation to join a club. Others of us turn down social invitations, genuinely preferring a quiet evening at home to mixing with a lot of people. Some of us would rather be left entirely alone with our thoughts or our books, but we are generally the ones who have too little time alone and think longingly of the joys of solitude.

But joining organizations and mixing with people are only superficial aspects of belonging. They are good, and are therefore satisfying and helpful to many of us. But they are not necessary. Those of us who are not "mixers" and who enjoy being alone do not need the reassurance of

superficial belonging because, consciously or not, our
security has its roots in the deep-down, rock-solid conviction that we belong.

Those whose basic sense of belonging is out of focus are
disturbed human beings. They are the unfortunates in our
mental hospitals, confused, wretchedly lonely, withdrawing
ever farther into themselves and losing contact with reality. Sometimes they can be brought back if their sense of
not belonging is self-imposed and has no basis in fact.
Sometimes they are beyond recall and unresponsive to all
the urgings of modern medicine and psychiatry, because
they have destroyed the lines of communication. Without
belonging we cannot *be.* That is, we cannot be what we
are meant to be. We can exist, but not as fully human beings.

"It is not good for man to be alone" God said in the Garden of Eden, when He created Eve to be Adam's companion. It is never good for man to be alone. It is so foreign
to his nature to be alone that he must perish unless he
knows himself as part of the whole in which he finds his
completion.

We belong, first of all, to God Who made us. Our belonging to Him is absolute. The fact that we may never give
Him a thought, or even be quite sure that we believe in
Him, does not lessen our utter dependence upon Him. God
could have limited our belonging to Himself alone, as He
does the angels. Instead, He made each of us part of a spe-
cies to which we belong, and set each of us at birth into a
family to which we belong in a more immediate and intimate way. So vital is our belonging that He gave us heav-
enly as well as human parents—for He is our Father and
His Mother is our mother in a parental relationship as real,
as immediate, and as practical as that which we have with
our earthly fathers and mothers. And He gave us two homes

in which to put down roots if we are to live and grow—our family home, and our spiritual home which is His home in our neighborhood.

Belonging is defined as being a part of, but human belonging means being a purposeful rather than an accidental part. "Working parts" might describe us better. An old silver spoon or an antique glass pitcher may belong to our collection, but they are accidental parts. They may make our collection more complete or more valuable, but our collection remains a collection without them, and they can perform their functions apart from the collection—we can still eat from the spoon and pour from the pitcher. The bobbin of our sewing machine is a working part. The machine cannot work without it, and we cannot use a bobbin apart from a sewing machine. But the analogy limps, as analogies do. We can always get another bobbin exactly like the one we lose, and it will contribute to the working of our sewing machine in exactly the same way. But human beings cannot be substituted, because each of us has a distinct contribution to make to the whole and, if we do not make it, the whole remains incomplete and we remain unfulfilled.

For belonging is not a passive, but an active relationship. It imposes responsibilities. Belonging completes us to the degree we help complete that to which we belong.

All of us are aware of belonging to our families, and know that our "belongingness" strikes its roots at home. That is why so many of us, in our middle and later years, feel lost and lonely when we are uprooted from home. And that is why God, in His wisdom, has given us a spiritual home that we can never lose. Wherever we find ourselves, that home is no farther than our nearest church. Wherever we find ourselves, we belong to a parish, and everyone in that parish is the family God has given us.

Listen next time someone asks you something about the parish. "*Your* parish," he'll call it, "*your* church, *your* school." Why? Because, quite simply, it *is* yours. All yours, from altar to holy water font, from the desks in the schoolrooms to the chairs in the rectory parlor. You helped build and furnish it, you help heat and clean it, you help support and maintain it. Or at least you should, because you benefit from it. Your parish exists for no reason under God's Heaven but to help you and your family and your fellow parishioners (and all within hearing distance of the Good News) to get to God's Heaven.

It is not just a place where necessary functions are performed, any more than your home is just a place where you eat, sleep and wash up. Your parish is your spiritual home, where you are born into God's family, educated, nourished, washed when you are unclean, healed when you are sick, comforted and counseled, married, enjoy the best of companionship, die in God's grace—and are loved more than you can know.

Your parish needs your financial support, as does your physical home. But, like your physical home, it needs more: your loyalty, your active interest, your cooperation, a portion of your time and effort. And, like your physical home, it returns you richer dividends on even a minor outlay than any other investment.

As parishioners, we belong to parishes. That's not so obvious as it sounds, because it depends upon what "belong" means to us. We don't belong to a parish as we belong to a club, where fulfilling our obligations is a simple matter of attending meetings and paying our dues. We belong to our parish as we belong to our family, and our obligation goes beyond mere presence at services and contributions in the collection plate; we have a share of the work to take over, other members to help and encourage and care for, and a lot of loving and praying to do.

A pastor cannot function with a single pair of hands, nor even with those of the faithful few who always offer their services. He needs the hands and hearts of everyone in the parish. He needs all of us, but much as he needs us, we need him more.

Something happened not long ago in my parish church that happens all too often in churches throughout the country. Only the details may differ. A man in the parish— I will call him John because that's not his name—stepped into the rectory and asked to see one of the priests. As he waited, he looked around curiously. Though he had passed the building every Sunday on his way to Mass, this was his first venture inside, impelled by the need of getting a small but important piece of information.

A pleasant young priest entered and greeted him. A few minutes' talk gave John the facts he needed and, after thanking the priest, he said:

"You're new here, aren't you, Father?"

Father's eyes twinkled. "Not what you might call *brand* new," he replied. "This June it will be four years. How about you—are you and your family recent arrivals in the parish?"

John had the grace to look embarrassed.

"No, Father," he said, "we've been here going on ten years. And we've been pretty regular with Sundays and holy days too."

To cover his confusion he gave Father's hand a bone-crushing shake.

"We must have missed each other," he said as he left. "Or you don't look the same. I guess vestments make a difference."

"Vestments aren't all," thought Father, as he watched John go.

The encounter left both men a little uncomfortable. Yet the priest could hardly have been expected to recognize a face that he could not recall seeing at any of the parish society meetings or social affairs. And since there had been no baptisms, marriages or funerals in John's family during the four years the priest had been in the parish, the name was unfamiliar to him. Nor did the name appear on the parish collection envelopes or the school register.

John, too, felt that his failure to recognize the priest was understandable. After all, it was a big church, the last Mass was always crowded, and it is hard to see a priest's face distinctly, even in the pulpit, from the last few rows. And though the Communion rail was a better vantage point, it was quite likely that another priest had said the Mass the few times a year that John received.

John's children did not attend the parish school. As for parish societies, John was pretty busy with an exacting job and too tired in the evenings to do anything except look for recreation. John's money went into the collection basket every Sunday, but it went in anonymously. He disapproved of the envelope system on two counts: if you didn't give much, it was nobody's business but your own; and if you did give a lot, the envelopes seemed to him a proud sort of self-advertising.

John considered himself a good Catholic. But what he (and many, many thousands like him) overlooked is the simple fact that *you cannot be a good Catholic without being a good parishioner.*

You cannot be good in general without being good in particular.

You cannot be a good Episcopalian or Baptist or Presbyterian or Jew without supporting your faith and working at it and worshiping God at regular times and at an appointed place along with the fellow members of your parish or congregation.

It is practical to remember that the same thing has happened to the parish dollar that has happened to our own; it is worth half of what it was. Meanwhile, the costs of maintaining the parish and running the school have at least doubled in the last decade, as have our own living costs. We should realize that most of the "money talk" we hear is the fault of those parishioners who can give and do not, and we should blame them instead of the pastor. Priests were not trained to beg for money, and should not have to. To a man, they loathe it. If they must, it is because we make them. And the ironic twist is that they must beg *us* for money to use for *us*—not for themselves!

If we have young children we should bring them up-to-date on this matter. Youngsters are smart about money. There is not one I know who does not turn up his nose at a nickel today. Nickel mentality is passé with the children— except at the children's Mass. A dose of the Golden Rule might help: what they do unto the church collection shall be done unto their allowances.

We should treat our pastor and his assistants like the fine friendly human beings they are, remembering that they *are* human. If we have a complaint, we should take it to the priest and not to the neighbors. There are fifteen thousand people in the average city parish; if we cannot always please one husband or one wife, we cannot expect the pastor to please fifteen thousand very different people, always and in everything.

If we especially like something, we can spread the word among the neighbors, but we should not forget to tell the priest too. He is a dedicated man who works for love—love of God and love of us. These days he is expected to be a welfare worker, a social organizer, a party arranger, a juvenile expert and a dozen other things besides a priest. He is expected to (and does) listen to woes from morning to night. He is not looking for praise. But he is still a man, and an occasional pat on the back is like a dozen helping hands to him.

We should weigh the natural limitations of the priest against what he gives us: absolution, counsel, the Blessed Sacrament, instruction, help in need, comfort in sickness, marriage, the last rites. We do not do so badly.

Belonging means standing up and being counted in our parish. It means using collection envelopes if they are provided, realizing that the pastor does not have them to see who gives what, but to know who is in the parish family and whom he can count on. It means showing up at parish social activities and at evening devotions once in a while. It means joining a parish society, remembering that our names on the roster (and even our dues in the till) cannot take our place at meetings. We need to be active members, because only if we are can we experience the enormous satisfaction of doing our share and come to know what parish societies really are: opportunities for service, for giving, for growing. There are many needs in every parish and we can often give more help as members of a parish society than we can as individuals.

"Wouldn't it be wonderful," one pastor told me, "to have a list, here at the rectory, of people who are willing to stay with the sick for an hour on Sunday mornings in order to allow those in charge of them to attend Mass! No more than two phone calls would be necessary. Someone would phone and say: 'I'd like to go to the ten o'clock Mass. Have you someone to stay with a sick person then?' And we'd phone a number on our list. *Real* charity is so simple, isn't it?—and so blessed."

Most churches look as if they are set squarely in the middle of a parking lot on Sunday mornings. If we take a tally of all those seats in all those cars, we will find that a good half of them ride empty. Lifts to church could become a big factor in raising the spiritual level of any parish, and raising our own as well.

Baby-sitting during Mass is on the increase, but it should increase until this service is available in all parishes. Sometimes high-school girls volunteer for this important service, but it's custom-tailored for those of us who are long past our high-school years, caring in shifts for babies and small children in the parish hall during all Sunday Masses and thus enabling young parents to attend Mass together without their youngsters competing with the priest for attention.

There is more, so much more, to be done; enough to keep the pastor worrying and praying far into every night. There is the matter of released-time instruction, which needs people to supervise the children, bring them safely from school and call on children who don't show up. There is the parish census. There are the parish delinquents (adult as well as juvenile), the fallen-aways. There are the newcomers and the converts to be welcomed and made to feel at home. There are the poor, the friendless, the hungry, the fathers out of work, the mothers who cannot afford to get sick because there is no one to look after the children.

Most of us Catholics are generous in support of our Church: we contribute regularly to our parishes, our dioceses, our charities and missions; we help support our seminaries and build schools and hospitals and orphanages. But we follow a rather strange and illogical pattern of generosity. It stops short at death, just when it would do us (as well as others) the most good. Either we forget God in our wills or we die without a will, and the state rules out God as a beneficiary.

Whatever our present age, making a will is not only important but an important obligation. It may come as a surprise to know that St. Francis de Sales laid down, as one of the first duties of a devout person, the early making of a will.

We shake our heads in wonder sometimes when we read accounts of a fortune being willed to a pet dog or cat, and the subsequent legal battles between relatives and Fido or Tabby for possession of the property. I think we should wonder more about those of us who live and die in the Church but forget her in our wills. And I think we should wonder most of all about those who forget the Church but have to scrape their memories to find distant relatives, not heard from in years, among whom to divide their property.

True, there are not many of us who lie awake nights wondering: "What shall I do with that extra $500,000 I have lying around?" It is equally true that there are some of us who, when our wills are opened, will be found to have left that much and more. But we can be just as generous with $50,000 or $5,000 or $500 as with $500,000. It's not the amount but the generosity that is measured in Heaven, the love with which it is given, and the sacrifice that made it possible.

There are four big mistakes that most of us make when it comes to wills. We do not make a will, thinking that we have not much to leave so it does not matter. We put off making a will, feeling that we have plenty of time. We do not have a lawyer draw up our will. And we leave God out of our will.

Let us see why they are big mistakes.

Even if we do not have much to leave, a will is important. It is not the amount we leave, but how we dispose of it that matters. Only we know how to divide our property fairly. Only we know the special needs to be met in the family, special circumstances not obvious to outsiders, special friends who deserve to be remembered. When we die intestate (without a will), the courts take over our property and divide it according to law. Hardship often results, sometimes even tragedy.

If we have been putting off making a will because "there's plenty of time," it might be wise to ask ourselves how we know. We are taking a chance on dying intestate, thereby causing those we love more misery than we realize. Or if we have been putting it off until we are older and may have more to leave, we should remember that a will, irrevocable after we die, can be changed easily and often while we live and as our circumstances change.

If we try to draft our own will we may defeat the very purposes for which we make it. Only a lawyer knows his way through the intricate requirements of the law which vary from state to state. Only he knows how to avoid all the mistakes and pitfalls that can invalidate our entire will, or cause the court to throw out certain of our bequests. It is our job to decide how we wish to dispose of our property. It is our lawyer's job (and only he can do it) to see that our will is so drafted that our wishes will be carried out.

God should be a beneficiary of every will, because the part we leave to Him is the part we *can* take with us. It will help others after we have gone, and it will help us *where* we have gone.

How to make a good will? We should first make a list of everything we own: money, bank accounts, securities, real estate, jewelry and the like. These things should be described so that they can be identified easily, and the location of each should be given. Then we list the people and organizations among whom we wish to divide our property. It is important to put down their correct names and addresses. In the case of organizations, it is particularly important to put down their *legal* names. Often the names by which they are popularly called are not their legal names. For example, the Paulist Fathers are well known, but their legal name is The Missionary Society of St. Paul the Apostle in the State of New York. Chances are that the legal name of our favorite charity is something other than what we call it. When our list is complete, we put down opposite the name of each the item or amount or proportionate share of our property to be given to that beneficiary.

We should decide upon a trustworthy and capable executor who will administer the property covered by our will, and choose him with great care. The duties of an executor are many and complex, so he should be both responsible and experienced in this special kind of work. Our lawyer or our bank might be a good choice.

Finally, we should take our lists to our lawyer, get his advice, and let him draw up a valid will that will stand up in court even if it should be contested.

Who should be remembered in a will?

First, our immediate family, according to its needs. In the case of distant relatives, there is no need to remember them just because they are distant. We may wish to remember them, however, if they have been close to us in friendship; or if we owe them a debt of gratitude.

Then come friends and loyal employees who deserve consideration, but who would not be given it by law if we died without a will.

We should remember our parish charities, our diocesan institutions and the Church's world-wide missionary needs. Do I sound as if I am getting up into that $500,000 bracket? I am not, except in the sense that $50 feels like $500,000 to some poor missionary half around the world, and $500 will build a chapel on the fringe of a jungle that will give as much glory to God as many a $500,000 church in

Suburbia, U.S.A. Our obligation to support the Church and to spread the Faith does not end at death.

Above all we should leave priests to the Church by leaving as much as we can afford, and a little more, to our diocesan seminary to help train and educate priests who are the very lifeblood of the Church.

Without priests we would have no Church. Without enough priests the Church cannot carry out her divine mission of salvation. Without many more priests than we have now the future of the Church in America's skyrocketing population is endangered. Educating a priest is a long and expensive process. In more normal times it cost about $10,000. Today it costs at least $20,000. That is a lot of money when you figure the things it can buy. But it is dirt cheap when you figure the things it *can't* buy: a single Holy Communion, a single absolution. It cannot buy them, but it can make them possible.

Matt Talbot, the alcoholic who gave up drinking for God, and for whose canonization a lot of people all over the world are praying, was not a rich man. He lived like a pauper all his life. But he worked all his life, too; he put in a full day's work the very day before he died. His pay was small, but it did big things. Matt Talbot spent his money to make priests. As priest after priest ascended the altar, aided by this poor man's sacrifice, you may be sure the name of Matt Talbot was spoken in Heaven.

Generosity with our worldly goods, while we live and when we die, is the kind of generosity that is repaid a thousand-fold. Generosity with our time and energy, as long as we are able, will repay us as richly. Our parishes need both. But above all parish needs, there is another that is most urgent of all: *parishes need prayers.*

Prayer is the lifeline of a parish, just as it is of an individual or of a family. We who belong in the true sense of belonging will get down on our knees regularly and storm Heaven with prayers for all the people within the confines of our parish, regardless of what faith they profess or if they profess none; for all who need our prayers so badly, and most especially for those among us who have forgotten how to pray.

Prayer is part of the most essential contribution we as individuals can make to our parish: *living in the state of grace*. That means showing up at the Communion rail regularly and often, and letting ourselves be filled so brimful with love of God that it spills over on our neighbors. Being in the state of grace is one thing, and living in it is another. If we flit in and out of it during our young and middle years, we shall follow the same pattern during our later years, to our eternal danger. But if we habitually live in it we shall have little need to worry. It is wise to remember that "deathbed repentances" occur mostly in fiction.

We cannot afford to be visitors to our spiritual home. We are family, we belong. To be good Catholics we have to be good parishioners. To be good parishioners we have to be good people. To be good people we have to work at saving our souls. Our priests, our Church, our parish are there to help. It is up to us to work with them, because the souls we are trying to save are our own.

XVII

The Powerhouse

We have been thinking together about all the activities that, started now, can grow with us into our later years and make them purposeful and satisfying because they help others as well as ourselves. In most cases they have been activities calling for at least some measure of strength and agility.

But suppose, in the day after tomorrow of our later years, we find ourselves with no strength, no agility? Suppose we are limited to bed or wheelchair and know pain as a constant companion? Suppose even now, in our young or middle years, we are invalided or crippled and live intimately with suffering?

We may feel that we are helpless to help others since we cannot help ourselves. If we do, we are terribly wrong. For those of us who suffer have within us a power to help others so mighty that it staggers our understanding. It is not an imaginary or vague sort of influence, but an actual force that is precise, powerful and that has been proved over and over again.

Those who suffer may feel that it is easy for those who do not to talk about it. It is not easy, because suffering is real and terrible, and those who are not presently suffering feel that they have little right to talk about it. But the fact of suffering exists, and the power of suffering is constantly being demonstrated.

The story of a little old lady who died just a year ago in Washington, D.C., at the age of eighty-eight, is one of these demonstrations. She had been paralyzed since her teens, had spent almost half a century in bed and almost a quarter of a century in a wheelchair. Yet so great was her love for the Christ Child that through seventy-one years of sleepless nights and pain-filled days, He worked through this "other Mary" to accomplish great things.

She was Mary Virginia Merrick, known and loved as "Miss Mary" to hundreds of thousands of the rich and of the poor. Her love for the Christ Child, which enabled her to see Him in every child, led to the formation of the Christ Child Society at her bedside in 1887. Since then it has grown to thirty-seven chapters in as many cities, with a membership of twelve thousand. Through the society, her love has provided clothes and recreation for thousands of poor children, sent them from city slums to fresh-air camps each summer, and helped convalescent children grow strong in the air and sunshine of the Christ Child Farm.

Miss Mary, one of eight children, was born into a distinguished Washington family on November 2, 1866, the year after Appomattox. Until well into her teens she was an active, fun-loving girl whose only fault was giving away her clothes and all her belongings to the poor children she met. When she was seventeen, she fell from a window and injured herself so severely that a paralytic condition set in. Medical science of the day was helpless to aid or even to advise. The family could afford the best doctors, but they had neither treatment nor suggestions to offer.

Miss Mary was confined to her bed through most of her adult life. It was not until she was about fifty that a steel brace was devised to support the upper part of her body so that she could sit in a wheelchair with a harness arrange-ment and leather support in which to rest her chin, for she could not hold up her head for long at a time.

Restricted to movement only with her hands, her keen mind and overflowing heart enabled her to pioneer in one of the most difficult fields of all: the care of sick and poor children. Her love for the Christ Child ignited one of the most complete child-welfare organizations in the country, helped her to inspire and direct it actively until her death, and enabled her to raise large sums of money for a gigantic building program which included settlement houses, sum-mer camps and convalescent homes.

Today, in addition to branches and facilities in thirty-seven cities, the Christ Child Society has a $100,000 settle-ment house in Washington and a $450,000 convalescent farm in nearby Maryland. Miss Mary, as president of the society, always felt it her personal responsibility to raise the combined budget of $150,000 for the two establishments. Two summers ago, in her wheelchair, she attended the Society's benefit garden party at the Brazilian Embassy which raised $10,000. A young girl worker, who didn't know Miss Mary by sight, approached her and asked if she would not like to sign up for membership in the Society.

"No, my dear," she replied, her eyes merry. Then she whispered confidentially, "I understand they work you too hard."

Now the Christ Child has taken Miss Mary home. But those who knew her feel that she will not take a well-deserved rest. If she could accomplish such great things while bound by bed, brace and wheelchair, they expect even greater things now that she has all of Heaven from which to operate.

Miss Mary and her work were not exceptional if by exceptional we mean something contrary to the usual. Because God constantly makes use of the little, the poor, the sick, the helpless to show forth mighty accomplishments and to show that they are from Him. That these accomplishments are often hidden does not make them the less mighty. The power of our suffering, if we put it to the right use, may not blossom into societies or building programs, but its results in souls will be just as astonishing. The secret lies in its right use.

The principle is a simple one: prayer alone is powerful, but *prayer backed by sacrifice or suffering is invincible.*

Prayer is always answered, and always for our good. Many of us have the odd idea that "Yes!" is the only answer to prayer, and that when we do not get what we pray for, our prayer has not been answered. We forget that "No!" is also an answer to prayer. But there is something further to remember: God desires only our good, and answers our prayers in the way that is good for us. It may take a long time for us to realize that something we prayed for would not have been at all the good it seemed. Even to pray that our suffering, or the suffering of another, be taken away may not be the good it seems, because God may well wish to bring about a greater good through that suffering. We should ask God for the things we want, but every prayer should include, if not in words at least in the spirit in which we pray, "Thy will be done." Because God's will is our only good.

Why pray at all then, if God's will is going to be done anyway? Because, unless we pray, it may not be done. Jesus told us to ask His Father for anything we wish, in His name. We are supposed to pray and to persevere in prayer. If we pray we will be answered, and our answer will be for our greatest good because it is God's will. If we do not pray, there will be no answer because there is no prayer to be answered, and things will take their course, possibly to our harm or to that of those about whom we are concerned. God's love and mercy keep flooding down upon us, and He often surprises us with great blessings even when we have not asked for them. But He does not simply hand us the specific things we want. We are supposed to ask for them.

Sacrifice and suffering add untold power to our prayers. We might almost say they "force God's hand" in our behalf. They do not, of course, persuade Him to do anything He does not will, anything that is not for our good. But when we pray that His will be done in any specific problem or need, and back it with our sacrifices or suffering, His answer is immediate, obvious to those concerned, and powerful beyond our imagining.

But sometimes we wonder about sacrifice and suffering, because they are two different things. Sacrifice is something we do voluntarily. Often it entails some suffering, but in any case it is something that we do of our own free will and so it is precious to God. Suffering, on the other hand, is not something we choose. There is not one of us who does not shrink from it. Since we are given no choice in the matter, in what sense can it be said that suffering is so precious to God that it can make our prayers invincible?

Suffering in itself is no more precious to God than it is to us. It is the use that we make of our suffering that is precious to Him and so powerful a help to us and to those around us.

Suffering is an individual matter. It is meaningless to talk about the tremendous amount of suffering in the world, because actually there is no more suffering than any single individual suffers. C. S. Lewis illustrates this truth with his usual clarity. "We must never make the problem of pain worse than it is," he says, "by vague talk about the 'unimaginable sum of human misery.' Suppose that I have a toothache of intensity x, and suppose that you who are

seated beside me also begin to have a toothache of intensity
x. You may, if you choose, say that the total amount of pain
in the room is now $2x$. But you must remember that no one
is suffering $2x$: search all time and all space and you will
not find that composite pain in anyone's consciousness.
There is no such thing as a sum of suffering. When we
have reached the maximum that a single person can suffer,
we have, no doubt, reached something very horrible, but
we have reached all the suffering that there ever can be in
the universe. The addition of a million fellow-sufferers adds
no more pain."

Suffering is something that is physically ours, and thus it
is ours to do with as we like. We can give it since it is ours to
give, not in the sense of giving it *away*, but in the sense of
offering it or applying it for our own purposes. We can accept it with patience, and offer it to God, so that He will
apply the merits of our acceptance and patience to our
prayers and thus give them force. Our acceptance and patience must stem from our loving confidence that God will
turn our suffering to His good purposes. We have heard that
God writes straight with crooked lines. He is able to turn
suffering, and even sin, into good.

But our suffering, severe as it may seem to us, is actually
very little. It is a little thing to offer so great a God, and it is
further weakened by our own human weaknesses. When we
offer it we are apt to wish that, just the same, we did
not suffer so much, or we might be tempted to bargain with
God, thinking that we "deserve" to get what we ask for because of our suffering. Alone it is not a great deal, but if we
accept it willingly as a small share of Christ's suffering on
the Cross, and offer it to God in union with His Son's offering of Himself for us, our little suffering takes on some of
the redemptive power of the Crucifixion, and Christ Himself
presents our prayers to His Father.

The power of suffering has proved itself through all the ages, and is helping little people do big things all around us today. We would be astounded if we knew how many of the things we acknowledge to be great accomplishments were made possible by little unknown powerhouses of prayer.

The Maryknoll Sisters are just one of the religious orders that are doing magnificent work all over the world, relieving misery and spreading the love of Christ among those who have never heard of Him. This young and vigorous American order has grown, in little more than forty years, from a handful of dedicated women to over a thousand of them, and from a single paper-cluttered room to foundations, schools, hospitals, social service centers, convents, and thatched huts in every part of the world. But the real secret of their mighty accomplishments lies in what they call their "powerhouse," a tiny group of cloistered Maryknoll Sisters which is the outgrowth of the Maryknoll spirit of prayer. They spend their lives in prayer and penance, cloistered within a small frame building, in order to speed the work of their active Sisters. This powerhouse is the heart of the whole big busy community, without which its enormous activity might well produce much fuss but little fruit.

Suffering with a supernatural intention has been compared to using a dynamo to produce power at Niagara Falls. Suffering without a supernatural intention is a shameful waste, just as Niagara Falls without a dynamo is simply water wasting away. The power of suffering is one that can be used by any sufferer, and it is being channeled to accomplish specific intentions by leagues of shut-ins in this country and in others, who unite their prayers and their sufferings in order to storm the gates of Heaven.

One such league recently organized on an international

basis consists of invalids who suffer willingly and pray for the conversion of the world. Each invalid "adopts" a priest in some other country than his own, and offers his life, prayers, joys, sufferings and even death for the priest's personal sanctification, intentions, work and for conversions in his apostolate. The invalid promises to keep on praying for him in Heaven. The members are not asked for money but simply for their prayers and sufferings that accomplish what money cannot. Priests apply to the league to be "adopted" and each is assigned an individual invalid to be his personal spiritual dynamo. Membership is open to invalids, incurables (the deaf, dumb and blind) and to the aged who are defined as being women over sixty and men over sixty-five.

Those of us who would like to unite our prayers and suffering in the special work of this league may write to Our Lady's Guild of the Sick, 43a Albany Street, Leith, Scotland. Or we might inquire about leagues of shut-ins here at home. In any case, we should remember that it is not necessary to join a league in order to accomplish tremendous things.

Though the power of suffering has been used throughout history, by religious and lay people alike, a recent and unique development among religious orders affords dramatic example of its use. Good physical health has always been a requirement of those seeking to enter religious orders, because physical health is necessary to do one's full share of the work. Yet there have always been ill and incapacitated people who have longed to dedicate their lives to God in religion.

It remained for a brilliant young woman to establish in France, in 1930, a religious order of women composed of the sick and infirm, to help make expiation for the sins of the world by continuing through the suffering of its members the work of Redemption begun on the Cross. The chronically ill and the handicapped, whatever their condition, are admitted if they are not over thirty years of age. The only exceptions are those with contagious diseases that might endanger the community, mental cases, and illnesses that are neurotic in origin.

The order is known as the Congregation of Jesus Crucified. Its rapid growth in membership, necessitating four priories or convents in France, is astonishing when it is remembered what a seemingly impossible handicap the very nature of the order appears to place in the way of spreading activity. Yet God has seen to its growth, and seen, too, our need for it in America. Just a few months ago the order made its first foundation in this country, the Regina Mundi Priory at Devon, Pennsylvania.

The convents are not, as you might suspect, even remotely like hospitals or nursing homes. They are happy busy places where the nuns, in addition to their prayers, do all the work for a household of from twenty to forty people. Every nun without exception is given her appointed work to do, if for only fifteen minutes a day. It is a moving sight indeed to see, for example, a completely bedridden nun reading aloud to a blind nun sitting by her bedside who transcribes it on a Braille machine. Each nun tries to conceal any suffering she is experiencing, and is not permitted to mention her health except to answer necessary questions by proper authorities. Upon entering, each leaves all thought of her health to the Prioress and the nursing-sister. Thus instead of a depressing sick-room atmosphere there is one of exquisite charity, a joy that spills over to visitors and an amazing sense of initiative and energy.

It is significant, I think, that the motto of the order is not the simple *Amen* of resignation, but the *Amen, Alleluia* of joyous acceptance. Ours can be the same. For a sufferer to live in the spirit of *Amen* is good. For him to live an *Amen, Alleluia* is Easter triumph. Such joyous acceptance joined to prayer can accomplish greater things than any of us dare to dream.

XVIII

—◆—

The Big Step

I HAVE KNOWN Hod for years. He is a native of the New England community where we vacation every summer. It is a thriving community. It is swamped with skiers in the winter as well as vacationers in the summer, and the natives have only a few weeks in the late fall and early spring to repair, repaint and restock after one onslaught in order to be ready for the next. Everyone "lives off" the visitors, which is perfectly legitimate because purple mountains and crystal lakes are their stock in trade, and it is a rare dollar indeed that is not marked "tourist."

But Hod has always been different. No tourist dollars have ever jingled in the pockets of his worn blue jeans. He has eked out a living logging up the mountain, working on the roads, repairing someone's roof once in a while. It is not that he has scorned the tourist dollars, but just that he has not known how to attract any. So when he broke his leg last winter, and had a long period of inactivity to look forward to (after all, seventy-year-old bones do not mend fast), his friends got busy.

"Hod," they said, "it just don't make sense living here right on the road and not having nothing to sell. Whyn't you sell honey from your bees? You're a great fisherman, too, and there's lots of fishermen come up this way. You could sell them bait. Put up a big sign, and you can sit right here and make a living."

Well, Hod reckoned it was worth a try. He got Bart over at the paint shop to make him a big sign, and he was in business. He had been in business for a couple of months by the time we came up in July. I met Hod at the hardware store one day, and asked him how business was going.

"It's not," he said. They don't waste words in those parts.

"Got your sign up?" I asked.

"Yep," he said.

"No customers?" I asked.

"Piddlin' few," he said. "I get some fishermen in all right, but nobody buys my honey."

A few days later we drove out Hod's way to buy some honey. We had bought honey from Hod for too many summers to count, and had our mouths all set for more. But when we got there we did not feel like honey after all. It was his sign. Oh, it was big enough and bright enough. In letters a foot high that could be seen half a mile down the road, the sign read: "WORMS & HONEY."

We bought some honey anyway, but we had a talk with Hod, too. He could not see the sense at first.

"People want worms, I got 'em," he said. "People want honey, I got it. Sign says so."

"But, Hod," we argued, "you've got to put your best foot forward. You may get customers for the worms, but you're driving your honey customers away. They lose their appetites."

"Hmmph," said Hod.

But he could not deny the figures. We persuaded him to take the sign down and put up two separate signs at a little distance from each other: "PURE HONEY FOR SALE" and "HOD'S BAIT GETS THE BIG ONES."

Hod's business improved considerably after that, so much

so that the morning we returned to town we were surprised to find a large crock of honey on our doorstep with a note: "Take this home with thanks there is no worms in it from Hod."

The crock is empty now and the honey only a sweet sticky memory, but Hod himself is very much on our minds. Because Hod, though it's been many years since he has seen the inside of the old yellow Congregational church in which he was brought up, has all unwittingly preached an eloquent sermon to us Catholics.

For we Catholics, whatever our age, have something to sell, too, and a solemn obligation to sell it. We have been given the job of attracting "customers" to the Faith. We are out to win non-Catholics and, like Hod, we find the going rough because our sign reads "WORMS & HONEY." The world can't see our honey for our worms—or, I should say, our worms destroy the world's appetite for our honey.

What the world sees is the tough part, not the reward, of being a Catholic. It *is* tough being Catholic—mighty tough. But the reward is so great as to be out of all proportion to the difficulty.

The shining reason for everything Catholics do and do not do, the stupendous reason for Catholics being Catholics is a simple one: love of God. The tough part is meaningless, empty, absurd without the sweet part. Without love of God fasts become mere diets, and mortifications take a sadistic turn. Without love of God charity becomes philanthropy and prayer a pious incantation. Without love of God there would never have been a Catholic Church and, as a consequence, no Christians anywhere.

Catholics are people who are in love. Some of them are tremendously in love, and these keep our world from crumbling into nothingness. Many of them are very much in love, and these are responsible for drawing others to share our treasure. But most of us are too little in love so we parade our medals and rattle our beads in a great show of piety, while we take our discipline with long faces and much fuss and are quick to complain to all who will hear that the Church is too strict. We, God help us, are publicity agents for the hardships because we have not yet learned how light love can make them.

We should not hide our discipline because it is necessary and it is good. But it is intelligible only in the light of its end, so we should give that end at least equal publicity.

We have not only a Father in Heaven, but a Mother too, and all the saints of all the ages as our personal friends. We do not go to church to hear about God, we go to church to be *with* God, and to share in the renewal of His sacrifice to save mankind. For Jesus is as actually present on our altars as He ever was on the roads of Galilee. Can you imagine how the world would flock to the spot if He were to appear on Broadway or Main Street? Yet the world does not suspect that He is the reason we Catholics jam-pack our churches many times over every Sunday morning, and drop in so often between times to "visit." Non-Catholics do not suspect because we do not tell them. We do not advertise our most precious Possession.

It is not just a matter of talking our Faith. More important, it is a matter of living our Faith. For spoken truth can be denied, but living truth cannot. It takes faith to understand many of the things we say about our religion. But it takes only a pair of eyes to see (if we let it be seen) that we have the security others are searching for, the peace of mind and peace of soul that our generation has lost, the love of neighbor that can come only from love of God. It should be (but too often is not) obvious that we Catholics are supremely happy people, because we have Heaven in our grasp, with God's own sacraments to smooth the road and speed the way. We have the crock of golden honey. We have only to open it and invite the world to feast.

Why, then, don't we show that we have what the world is searching for? Some of us do, of course, but not enough of us. Some of us hoard these possessions for our own enjoyment. Some of us have them buried so far under worldly concerns that on the surface we appear as jittery and insecure and unhappy as everybody else. And some of us have allowed them to become rusty and ineffective through neglect of their Source. It amounts to the same thing. For whether a room is dark or brightly lighted but with dark shades drawn, there is no gleam of light to guide the outsider.

The statement: "I know nothing about Catholicism but I do know Catholics," has been made so often, by so many non-Catholics, that it has attained the dubious stature of a cliché. But, if you think about it, it contains a terrifying responsibility for Catholics; each one of us is, to more non-Catholics than we realize, not merely "a Catholic" but *the Catholic Church.*

Each of us is surrounded daily by a horde of silent witnesses who judge the Church, and receive or reject it, by what they see in us. An uncomfortable feeling? It should be uncomfortable. It should also be challenging. And most of all it should be satisfying, because giving good example, letting the Faith that is in us be seen in our lives, is the easiest yet most effective of all apostolates. We do not have to *do,* we simply have to *be.*

This is the apostolate to which we are called, the one for which we train today and tomorrow, in order that it may bear fruit the day after tomorrow, and in doing so not only give meaning to our later years but also justify them.

I remember a brilliant professor we had in college during the years before I became a Catholic. His mind was like a steel trap, his learning awed us to silence, his name was almost legendary even outside academic circles. One Saturday afternoon, caught in a sudden downpour while shopping, I stopped at St. Francis Church in midtown New York, and had to catch the back of a pew to steady myself at the sight of our brilliant professor, dripping hat in hand, standing humbly in a long line outside one of the confessional boxes.

"Surely," I thought, when I was able to think, "he is *above* things like that!"

And then, a long time later, I thought: "He is not above things like that. He is only above people like me. If he knows so much more than I do, and this is one of the things he knows, then I must learn it too."

The professor could have presented the case for his faith with breathtaking eloquence and invincible logic. To me, at least, he presented it more effectively by just going to confession.

When I first became a Catholic, and the wonder and beauty and glory of my new faith pretty nearly shattered me (for no one had warned me how terrifying is the first touch of truth), a question started tugging at the corners of my mind. I did not stop to examine it, I was so absorbed in the fresh realizations that kept bursting like fireworks all around me. But it kept tugging until it gave me no peace and I had to face it.

"Why," I had to know, "*why*—out of all my non-Catholic family, out of all my good non-Catholic friends—why did God choose *me* for His tremendous gift of Faith?"

It just did not make sense, yet I knew that God always makes sense. I had done nothing to deserve such a gift. I was, quite honestly, the most unlikely choice of all the non-Catholics I knew. It took plenty of prayer to arrive at the only possible answer: God gave me His true Faith, not just for my own use, but *to use it for Him.*

That is why we Catholics are Catholics, cradle and convert alike. For born Catholics do not inherit the Faith along with blue eyes or big ears. It is a free gift of God to each individual soul. And since it is God's greatest gift it is our greatest responsibility.

The apostolate of good example is not *doing* a lot of things. It is simply *being* one thing: a complete Catholic. When the mounting years impose their limitations, and little by little we start being whittled down to size, we will find that we will be able to do less and less. Some of us may be able to do little or perhaps nothing. But we can always *be.* The kind of person we grow to be during our busy years, the kind of person we become in our later years, is the kind of person we shall be through eternity.

A complete Catholic is a positive Catholic. A minimum Catholic is a negative one. A non-Catholic can see, in a minimum Catholic, only negatives. He cannot be blamed for concluding ours to be a religion of "nots": We cannot eat meat on Friday, we cannot miss Mass on Sunday, we cannot go to a non-Catholic church, we cannot get married at City Hall, we cannot get divorced, and so on down the dismal list. Is there anything we *can* do? We are against Communism, against "Planned Parenthood," against euthanasia, against secret societies. Aren't we *for* anything?

A negative can only repel. It takes a positive to attract. And there is no attraction more positive or more powerful than the silent apostolate of a fully Catholic life. It is so positive that there is no turning from it. It is so powerful that it can pull a non-Catholic from everyone and everything he holds dearest, and deposit him on his knees before God's altar, bruised from the bitterness he has had to fight, shattered by the sacrifices and separations he has had to endure, alone and yet never alone again.

Unlike all other religions ours is not just a creed of beliefs, nor a code of commandments. Our religion is a *Person* —a living Person, Who lives in us. Jesus Christ is not merely the reason we are Catholics. *He is the reason we are.*

We who feel that we have the Faith too often forget that the proof of having something is the ability to give it. When we hoard the grace that has been given us, we forget that we were never meant to be sealed flasks of faith, but open channels through which faith can flow to others. We shelter our little sparks lest they go out, forgetting that sheltered sparks are smothered and die. They must spread to unignited material to start a conflagration; from one to another in ever-widening circles until all the world is warmed and lighted by the fire of God's love. Faith is contagious, but a contagion needs carriers.

Our Faith is as practical as it is positive. Praying for our daily bread is a practical request that receives a stupendous but utterly practical answer in the Bread that God becomes for us every morning upon our altars. God hears that "daily" and supplies it daily. If we mean what we pray, we will receive it daily. Daily Mass and Communion, all our lives, make a difference that cannot be guessed at or imagined, but must be experienced. It is a difference as practical and positive as the pews we sit in, but a lot more lasting. Complete Catholics are formed, and the apostolate of good example is fired, at the altar rail. Souls are saved, and the world is changed, and Heaven is won, for all of us, by daily Communion. It is not strange to say that everything is accomplished in Communion, when we remember that Communion is everything. This is the essential preparation for the day after tomorrow, because it is essential for the day after that.

When we hear a hurried "Blessed Mother!" from the lips of a harried housewife, or catch the glint of a Miraculous Medal on a brawny chest at the beach, or glimpse a rosary in the purse of an office co-worker as she digs for lunch money, we label such a person "Catholic." It is a proud, triumphant label for us. It is too big a label for most of us. And because we are so little and the label looks so big, we hang it on Mary, thinking to honor her. Thus, day after day, we who love her most hurt her most.

For Mary is not Catholic. She is catholic. She is our mother, but she is as truly the mother of every man who ever lived: Protestant, Jew, Communist, bigot, or bush native. These others are her lost children, and we who have found her will not help her in her search for them.

Devotion to Mary is a striking Catholic characteristic. Lack of devotion to her is just as striking a characteristic among non-Catholics. The great majority of non-Catholics are sincere in what they believe. One man's belief may not match another's, but at least each has his beliefs about God and what is necessary for salvation, and is sincere about them. But this is a strange and wonderful sign of our security: it is possible for a man to believe what he likes about God so long as he does not admit the Blessed Mother into the picture. But it is impossible for a man to admit the Blessed Mother, and still keep his own private beliefs where those beliefs are at variance with Catholic teaching. *It is impossible for anyone to have a real devotion to Mary, and remain outside the Catholic Church.*

Therefore the question is not: "Why don't non-Catholics acknowledge Mary?" but "How can we bring non-Catholics to Mary?"

This is where we fail. We act like small children trying to attract our mother's undivided attention. We consider her as much Catholic property as the vestments in our sacristy or the pipe organ in our loft. She longs for her other children, who were given to her by Christ Himself from the Cross, but we join our little selfish hands in a ring around her to close her in.

It is said that when Louis Budenz, long-time Communist, agreed to have dinner with Bishop Fulton Sheen, he was eager to discuss Communism. But Bishop Sheen said that *he* wanted to talk about the Blessed Mother—and that he did, for an hour and a half. The rest is history. Give Mary so much as a man's coat-tail, and he finds himself deposited in the Catholic Church. All she asks of us is an introduction.

But we cannot introduce her to others if we are too busy to give her more than a hurried greeting ourselves. Nor can we come closer to God, and thus closer to the kind of people it is so important for us to be when the years close in around us, unless we take time to do so. Yet, despite all the time-saving devices that modern science has engineered for us, time seems to be the one commodity we do not have any more. Time to sit quietly and think things out. Time to talk to God and to get His slant on ourselves and our problems. Time to remember who we are, and why we are here, and where we are going.

Today we are so busy with so many concerns, beset with so many anxieties and tensions, confused by so many crowds and so much clamor, that we feel we are on a merry-go-round.We keep going at a dizzy pace and do not dare let go. But it's awfully hard to keep any sense of direction on a merry-go-round. We have to get off at regular intervals, and step away from it, in order to see its place in God's plan for us, and to see where He is pointing. Everything crowds up on us so fast these days that we have to retreat. And that is just what hundreds of thousands of us are doing.

We are retreating, to get our bearings and renew our strength, in order that we may advance more quickly and surely in the right direction. Retreats—weekends spent away from the world in some quiet convent or monastery—were born of dire necessity, and have grown because the need has grown. Precisely because America is the busiest place in the world today, the gigantic spread of retreats is a peculiarly American phenomenon. It is the life-saver we have had to fashion for ourselves, and to which increasing numbers of us cling.

The spectacle of so many hundreds of thousands of Catholics rushing off on retreat (and of increasing thousands of non-Catholics making Catholic retreats) is such a contradiction to the age we live in that it gives rise to a mammoth *why?*

The answer must be obvious even to outsiders. We live at a faster pace in America today than do the inhabitants of any other country in the world. Our lives are so hectic and so filled with busy confusion that even the time we allot to relaxation is at best a change of pace—but just as busy a pace.

We know that we can do nothing to change our dizzy pace, because it has long been out of our control. We know that time to think—to be still and know God (for He is found only in silence) and in knowing Him find ourselves and our direction again—doesn't just happen any more. We have to make time, seize it, wrench it right out of our busy lives, and retreat with it to a quiet place where we can let God do the talking.

Retreat houses have been called vestibules to Heaven. It is a beautiful thought and entirely true. But it is equally true today to call retreat houses spiritual emergency wards. They are meeting, as best they can, a very real and a very great emergency. For it is just plain fact that if the Faith is to be preserved and solidified in America, every American Catholic must get off the merry-go-round at least once a year every year, shut out the world, and see things once more in their proper perspective.

I have come to a retreat house for these final few hours of "thinking aloud" about our day after tomorrow. I have brought along with me the quietest typewriter I could find, and a thick sound-absorbing pad to put under it, so that my thinking will not be loud enough to disturb the thinking other retreatants are doing. I have been coming here, to the Cenacle, each year for as long as I can remember, and I find that each visit quite literally gives me the strength I need for the year ahead.

The original Cenacle, you remember, was the upper room where the apostles and the women gathered with Mary, the Mother of Jesus, after He had risen from the dead and been among them for a while and they had watched Him ascend into Heaven. They talked about Him, remembering the things He had done and the things He had taught them. They listened to His Mother recalling all the things He wanted them to do. He had sent them forth to preach the Good News to all the world, but these few unlettered men to whom He had entrusted so mighty a mission were afraid. So they spent the days quietly in that upper room, persevering in prayer with Mary. And on Pentecost the Holy Spirit came down upon them like a fresh and roaring wind, and touched each of them with a tongue of fire, and sent them forth with the courage that was to convert the world.

I am now in that "upper room." Only the details differ: my typewriter, my comfortable bed, the dining room to which a bell summons me to meals, the chapel which is the heart and meaning of it all. But the essentials have not changed. Mary is here and so is her Son.

A retreat is not a weekend spent thinking about Mary,

but a weekend spent with Mary. It is not a weekend wishing we were closer to God, but a weekend of being close to Him. If you have never before slept under the same roof with the Blessed Sacrament, as you do on retreat, you have a wonderful surprise coming: you sleep like a baby, and wake new born.

I am glad I came here to write this last chapter, because the answer is here. I can see it in the faces of the other retreatants: young women who have put all the questions that lie ahead of them into Mary's keeping, middle-aged women who have brought along their problems and have found to their delight that problems have a way of evaporating when seen through God's eyes, and old women filled with the peace of Heaven's anteroom and awaiting with joy the summons they will soon hear.

A retreat is a preparation. All through life it is the way we prepare for an important step. In our Catholic schools and colleges we go on retreat to prepare for graduation. Many of us go on retreat before we marry or to decide our vocation in life. Priests and nuns go on retreat before they enter the religious life, and regularly thereafter that they may deepen that life.

But all these steps, important as they are, are only steps we take through life toward the most important step of all. And though all of life is a preparation, our later years are a particular preparation because the Big Step is the only step that remains.

That is why, I think, God makes a retreat of our later years. If we have been too active, He limits us physically to slow us down. If we have been too filled with worldly concerns, He dims our sight or hushes our hearing to close out the world. He gives us the time to think that we have somehow never been able to make for ourselves. He bids us listen to Him in the quiet of our day after tomorrow.

It is strange how different things are when they come close to us. We see our lives stretching ahead, and when we have looked ahead as far as we can we think we see the end. But if we have walked the long road with faith and love, and finally arrive at what we have always imagined to be the end, we discover it is only

THE BEGINNING